THE · CHILDREN'S
Visual Dictionary

Written by
Jane Bunting

Illustrated by
David Hopkins

DORLING KINDERSLEY
LONDON · NEW YORK · STUTTGART

A Dorling Kindersley Book

Editor's Note

The Children's Visual Dictionary is packed with stunning picture definitions of a fascinating collection of words. Themes as diverse as *Mammals* and *Space* introduce children to a wide range of words, many set in descriptive phrases, including less familiar words that identify the special features of the objects illustrated.

Encourage children to learn how to use the book by looking up themes that appeal to their interests. The colorful photographs and illustrations will reinforce their understanding of new vocabulary and, with your help, they will relate themes to their own experiences and begin to use the words in conversation. In addition, the special word-finder index will help children learn to locate information that is organized in alphabetical order, allowing them to use many other reference books, from telephone directories to encyclopedias. The index will also serve as a quick spelling guide when writing.

This dictionary has been specially developed for young readers and writers, but, with adult help, pre-readers can benefit from the book as well. Naming and comparing the clearly labeled images aloud will encourage young children to associate each image with the written word, one of the first steps in learning to read.

The Children's Visual Dictionary is a language resource that will grow with a child, providing both a rich source of information about the world and a valuable resource for building reading and writing skills.

Project Editor   Monica Byles
Assistant Editor   Fiona Campbell
Art Editor   Peter Radcliffe
U.S. Editor   Camela Decaire
Managing Editor   Jane Yorke

Managing Art Editor   Gillian Allan
Production   Louise Barratt
Picture Research   Fiona Watson
Photography   Paul Bricknell,
                  Steve Gorton

First American Edition, 1995
2 4 6 8 10 9 7 5 3 1

Published in the United States by
Dorling Kindersley Publishing, Inc., 95 Madison Avenue
New York, New York 10016

Library of Congress Cataloguing-in-Publication Data

Bunting, Jane.
    The children's visual dictionary / written by Jane Bunting : illustrated
by Dave Hopkins. — 1st American ed.
        p.   cm.
    Includes index.
    ISBN 1-56458-881-5
    1. Picture dictionaries. English—Juvenile literature.
[1. Vocabulary.]   I. Hopkins, Dave. ill.   II. Title.
PE1629.B86   1995
423'. 1—dc20
                                94-29950
                                CIP
                                AC

Reproduced by Colourscan, Singapore
Printed and bound in Italy by Graphicom

Contents

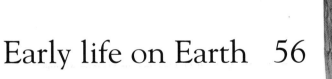

All about people

Human beings are special – we are the most highly developed mammal, and the only kind of animal to use words to talk to each other. Our brains control our bodies, allowing us to move quickly or slowly, think and remember, and express how we feel. As we grow up, our bodies gradually develop and change.

My family

father mother cousin brother aunt me

My feelings

feeling shy

loving my puppy

twin sisters   smile

feeling happy

tears

feeling sad

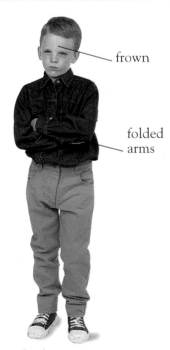

frown

folded arms

feeling angry

feeling excited

Parts of the body

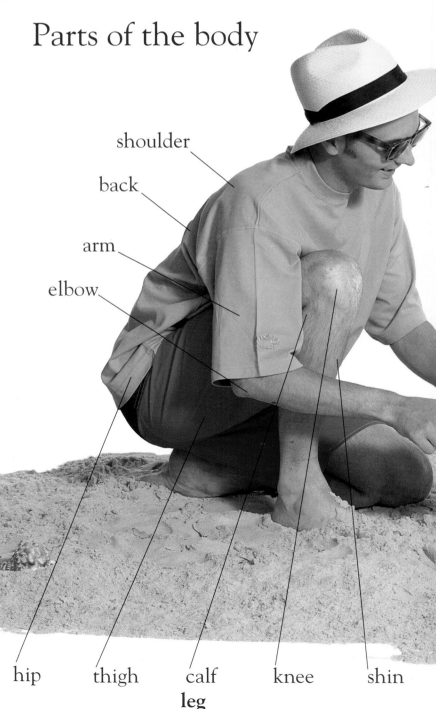

shoulder

back

arm

elbow

hip   thigh   calf   knee   shin

leg

Growing up

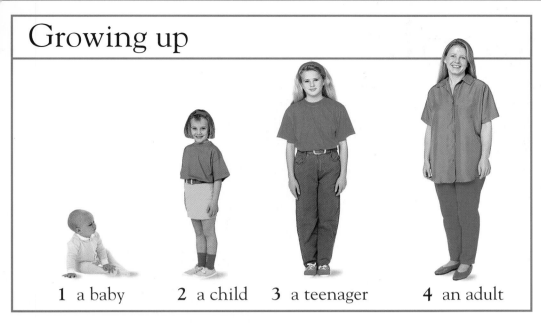

1 a baby **2** a child **3** a teenager **4** an adult

Sick in bed

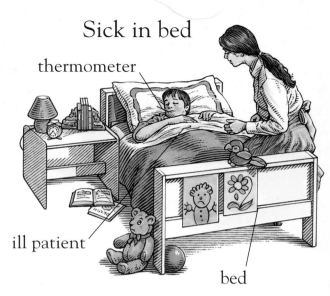

thermometer

ill patient

bed

face

eyebrow
forehead
eyelid
eyelashes
cheek
nostril
lips
chin

waist

belly button

head

hair
ear
nose
mouth
neck

toe ankle index finger thumb wrist

foot **hand**

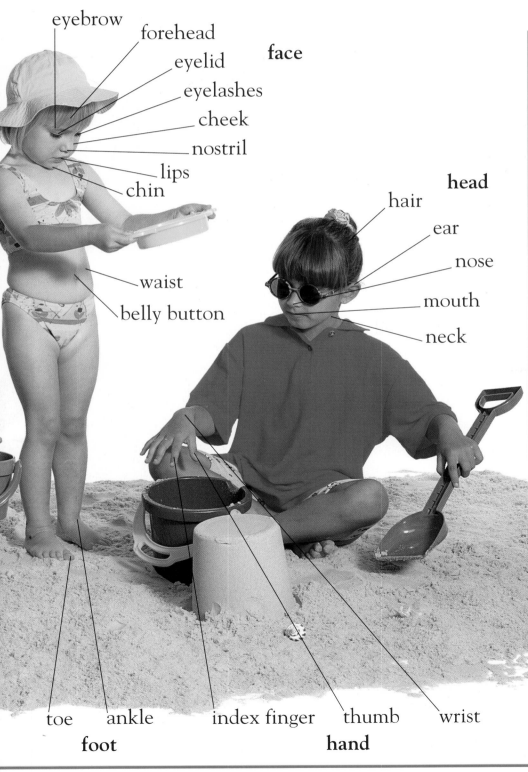

The five senses

nose

smelling flowers

hand ear

hearing a whisper

mouth

tasting a banana

shielding the eyes

seeing a long way

stroking soft fur

touching a cat

5

Going to school

In most schools around the world, teachers give lessons to classes of children. At school, children learn to read and write, and gain other skills and knowledge that they will need to live and work as adults. Schools also teach sports and recreational activities.

In the classroom

painting

wall chart

student   desk   workbook

At school

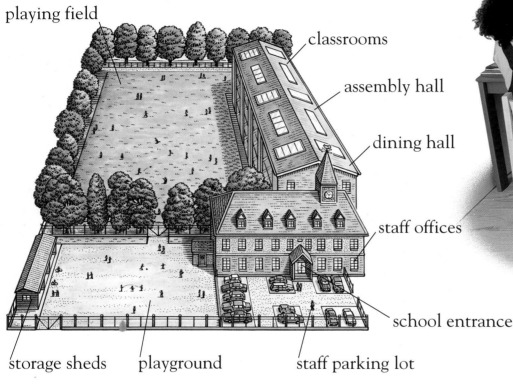

playing field

classrooms

assembly hall

dining hall

staff offices

school entrance

storage sheds   playground   staff parking lot

School activities

textbook

looking at books in the library

coach

sandpit

trying the long jump in a sports meet

doing a science experiment

electrical circuit

castle

building a model

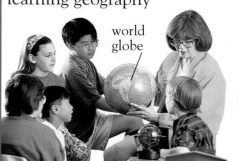

learning geography

world globe

6

resource
area

project work
on display

bulletin board

supply cart

teacher

Finding out

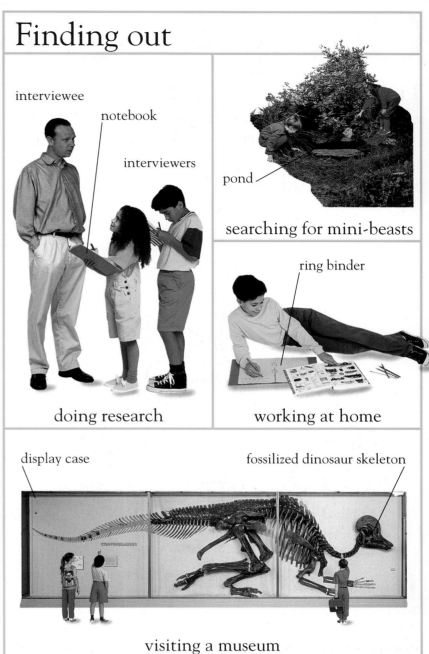

interviewee

notebook

interviewers

doing research

pond

searching for mini-beasts

ring binder

working at home

display case

fossilized dinosaur skeleton

visiting a museum

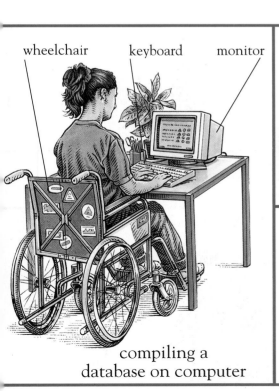

wheelchair

keyboard

monitor

compiling a
database on computer

compass

pencil

calculator

solving a math problem

curtains

stage set

stage

audience

putting on a school play

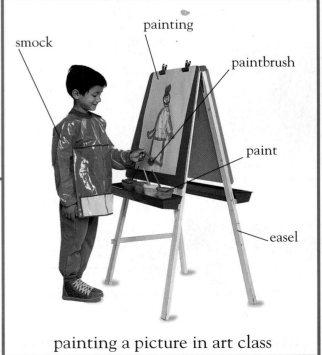

smock

painting

paintbrush

paint

easel

painting a picture in art class

People at work

M ost people work so that they can pay for food, clothing, and a home for themselves and their family. There are many different kinds of jobs, some outdoors, and some indoors in places such as factories and offices. Workers such as doctors and firefighters help people in need.

At the vet's clinic

veterinary assistant

lab coat

uniform

apron

pet dog

At the building site

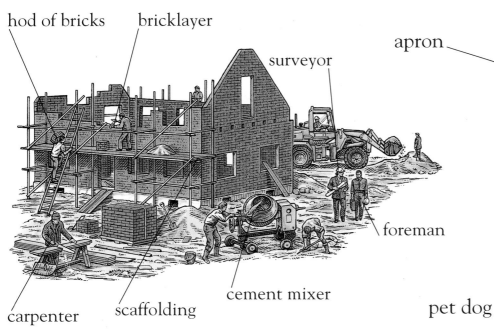

hod of bricks

bricklayer

surveyor

foreman

cement mixer

scaffolding

carpenter

Different jobs that people do

bouquet of flowers

a florist in a flower store

chef's hat

frying pan

a chef in her kitchen

swivel chair

computer

desk

an accountant in her office

oxygen tank

water nozzle

firefighters putting out a fire

microscope

lab coat

a scientist in a laboratory

veterinarian

pet owner

stethoscope

In a television studio

actress in costume

actor

makeup designer

television monitor

camera operator

director

sound recordist

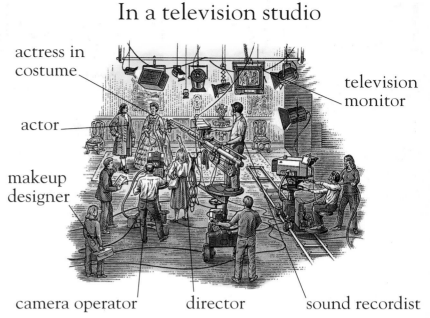

Medical professions

dentist

mask

in the dental chair

patient

doctor

at the doctor's office

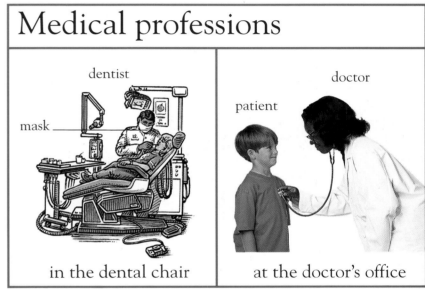

a hairdresser in his salon

scissors

comb

hair clips

potter's wheel

bin of clay

a potter in his studio

overalls

tool bag

a plumber with her tool kit

screwdriver

foreman

car engine

assembly line worker

conveyor belt

car factory workers on an assembly line

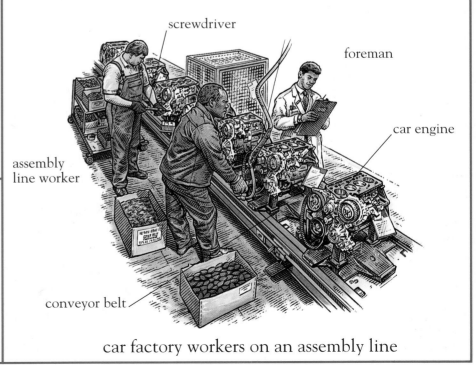

Going shopping

People shop for things that they want or need, such as food or clothing. At open-air markets, goods are sold from individual stalls. Specialized shops, such as bakeries or hardware stores, sell only one type of merchandise. At supermarkets and department stores, shoppers can find everything they need under one roof.

A busy fruit and vegetable market

vendor

weighing scales

shopping bag

customer

money

A shopping mall

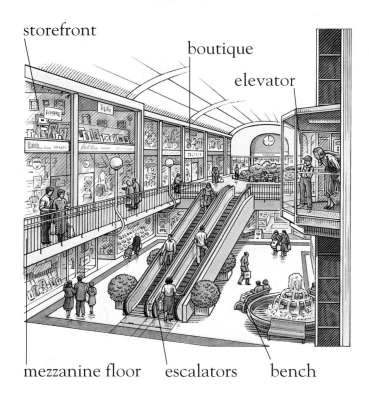

storefront

boutique

elevator

mezzanine floor   escalators   bench

A variety of stores

piled goods at a hardware store

cash register

checkout cashier

shopping cart

conveyor belt

in line at a supermarket checkout

cold meats

food case

selecting food in a delicatessen

leaving a bakery store

shopper

storage basket

fresh produce

price marker   shopping basket   crate

Customers in a toy store

store clerk

merchandise

sales counter

shoppers

soft toy   display shelves

Shopping essentials

coin

a purse for change

straw sack

a shopping bag

bills   credit cards

wallet for money and cards

notepad

pencil

a shopping list

designer furniture

a display in a furniture showroom

newspaper

vendor

buying a paper at a newspaper kiosk

clothes rack

clothes hanger

browsing in a clothing store

computer terminal

brochure

travel agent

customer

planning a vacation in a travel agency

Food and eating

All living things need food to stay alive. Food gives you energy, keeps your body warm, and helps you grow. People enjoy eating many different kinds of food, both raw and cooked. It is important to eat plenty of fresh fruit and vegetables and to have regular meals every day to stay healthy.

An outdoor café

umbrella

order pad

pitcher

diner

menu

waiter

A picnic

bottle of water

thermos

bowl of chips

pitcher

glass of juice

plate of sandwiches

napkin

picnic blanket

grilled sausages

Food and drink

garnish   crispbread

a delicious snack

chopsticks

some steaming rice

drinking straw

fruit pudding   teaspoon

saucer

a creamy dessert

a crunchy salad

citrus juicer

fresh orange juice

shrimp   skewer

a tasty seafood kebab

sparkling apple juice

seeds

a juicy melon

barbecue grill tray

a sizzling fish

picnic basket

fork knife plate spoon

bunch
of grapes

strawberry

pineapple

salt and
pepper
shakers

mug

bowl
of salad

**selection of
fresh fruit**

Cooking food

a chef chopping
vegetables

white coat

chopping knife

cutting board

pot apron

stirring some soup

kitchen
scale

measuring flour

dough

cookie
cutter

mixing
bowl

cutting out cookies

saucepan air bubbles

boiling some peas

baking tray

oven mitt

baking a cake

Tastes and flavors

sliced
pepper gravy

a savory meat stew

cream black cherry

a slice of sweet cake

salty peanuts

pith

lemon peel

sour lemons

whisk

whipping some cream

peeler

peeling an apple

Hobbies and pastimes

People relax and spend their free time in many different ways, either on their own or with family and friends. Many often choose to go out for entertainment, maybe to watch a movie or go to the theater. People also enjoy playing sports or exercising outdoors, but sometimes people prefer to simply practice a hobby at home.

A puppet show

puppet theater

audience

An outdoor challenge course

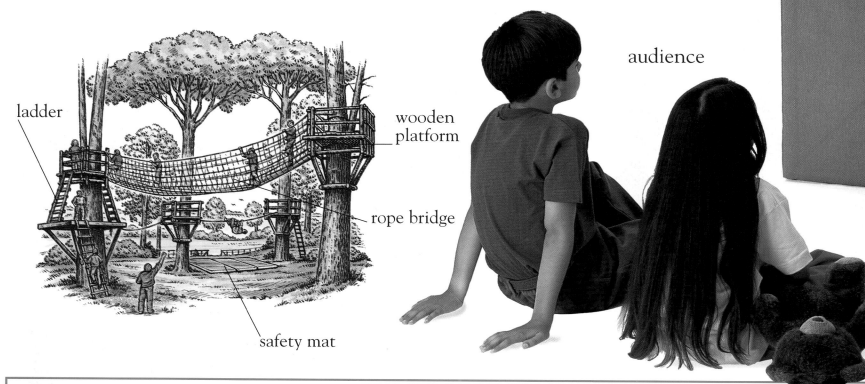

ladder

wooden platform

rope bridge

safety mat

Outdoor activities

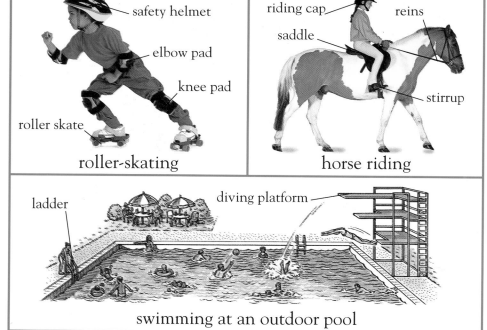

safety helmet

elbow pad

knee pad

roller skate

roller-skating

riding cap

reins

saddle

stirrup

horse riding

ladder

diving platform

swimming at an outdoor pool

tent

backpack

sleeping bag

flashlight

gas lamp

camping

backdrop

curtains

hand puppet

foreground scenery

stilt walker

juggling rings

juggler

stunt cyclist

stilts

unicycle

clown

Indoor activities

sneakers

dancing for fun

tiara

dressing up

reading a book

seat

wide screen

watching a movie

counter

dice shaker

board game

playing a game

tissue paper

scissors

making a collage

controls

playing a computer game

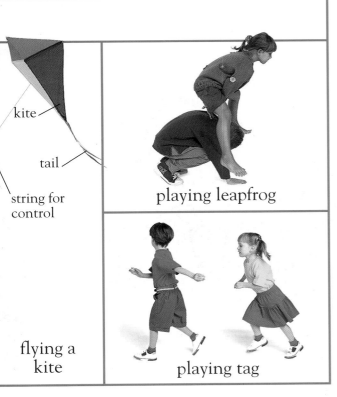

kite

tail

string for control

flying a kite

playing leapfrog

playing tag

15

Music

People around the world play many different kinds of musical instruments, on their own and together in bands and orchestras. Depending on how they produce sounds, musical instruments are grouped into families – string, woodwind, percussion, brass, keyboard, and electronic. Musicians either play written music, or improvise (make up the music) as they play.

Brass instruments

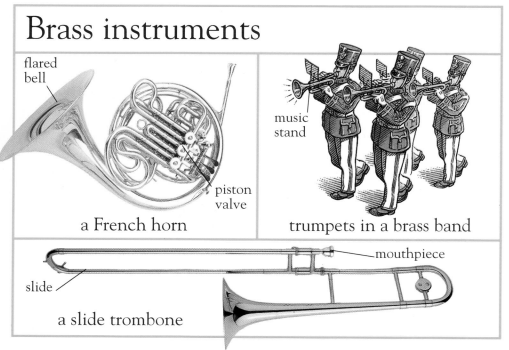

flared bell

piston valve

a French horn

music stand

trumpets in a brass band

slide

mouthpiece

a slide trombone

Some percussion instruments

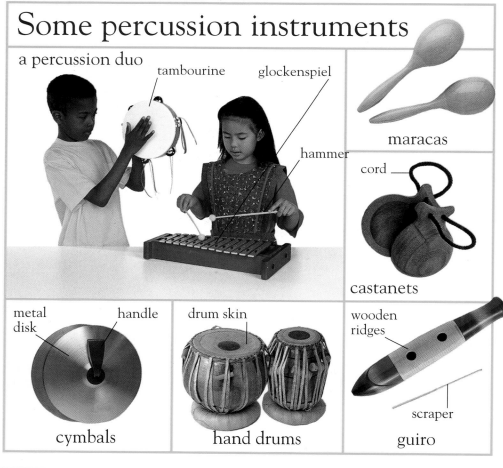

a percussion duo

tambourine

glockenspiel

hammer

maracas

cord

castanets

metal disk

handle

cymbals

drum skin

hand drums

wooden ridges

scraper

guiro

A violin

point

scroll

tuning peg

neck

string

hairs

stick

bow

frog

belly

screw

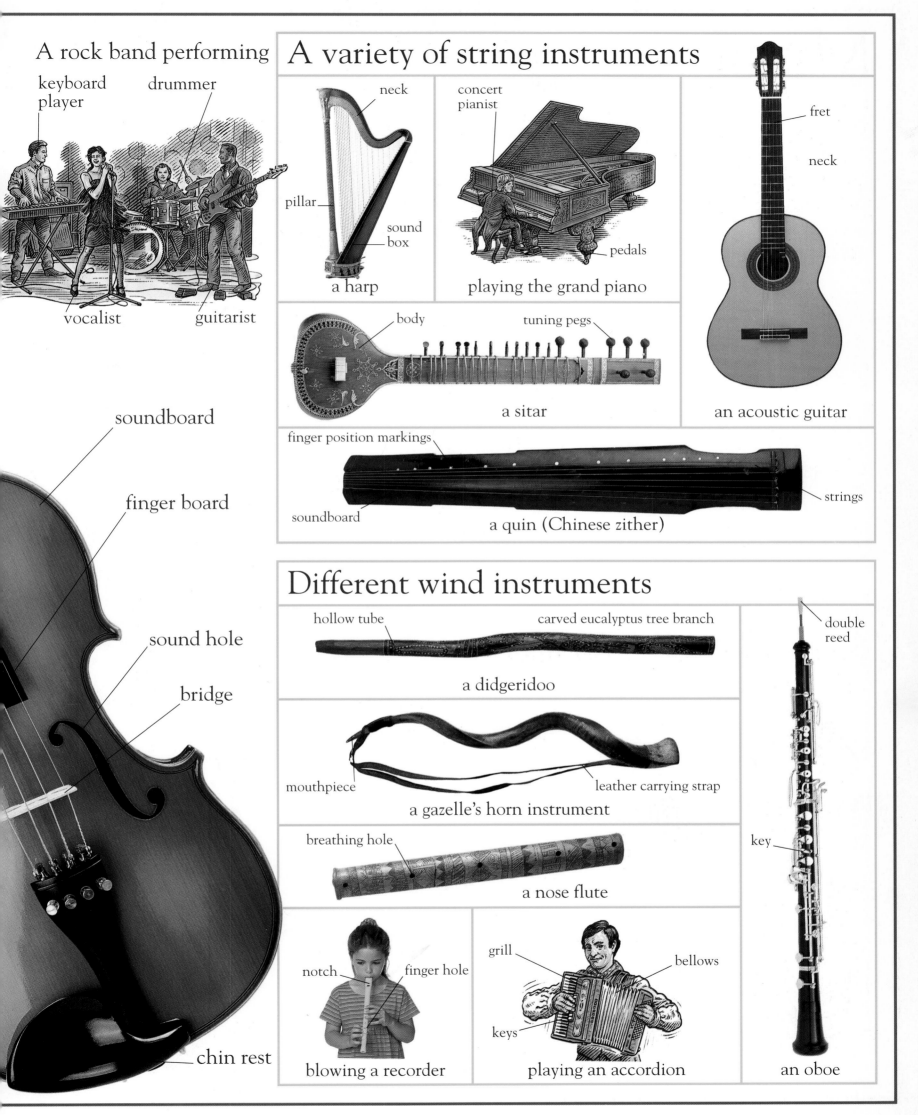

A rock band performing

keyboard player

drummer

vocalist

guitarist

A variety of string instruments

neck

pillar

sound box

a harp

concert pianist

pedals

playing the grand piano

fret

neck

an acoustic guitar

body

tuning pegs

a sitar

finger position markings

soundboard

strings

a quin (Chinese zither)

soundboard

finger board

sound hole

bridge

chin rest

Different wind instruments

hollow tube

carved eucalyptus tree branch

a didgeridoo

mouthpiece

leather carrying strap

a gazelle's horn instrument

breathing hole

a nose flute

notch

finger hole

blowing a recorder

grill

bellows

keys

playing an accordion

double reed

key

an oboe

Sports

Sports have been played for thousands of years. Players follow rules for each sport, and often use special equipment. In some sports, people try to beat other people's records. Many sports are team games, in which two sides compete.

Sports equipment

pocket baseball
lacing

a baseball glove

lace
blade

an ice skate

weights metal bar

a barbell

a basketball

laces cleats

a running shoe

strings
shuttlecock

a badminton racket

jacket

wet suit

a wet suit for windsurfing

face mask

a football helmet

a football

A sports stadium

grandstand playing field
spectator stands

entrance ticket office

saddle

back wheel

spoke

sprockets (gears)

derailleur

valve

a mountain bike

chain ring

chain

A soccer match

goal goalkeeper

attacker

soccer ball

defender

18

A cyclist

- helmet
- chin strap
- handlebars
- gearshift
- brake
- front wheel
- hub
- frame
- pedal
- tire

Ball games

cricketer

cricket bat

batting in a cricket match

basket

shorts

basketball player

scoring in basketball

tennis racket

forehand shot in tennis

tennis sneaker

baseball bat

ready for the pitch in baseball

Track-and-field events

judge

high jump

sprint

javelin throw

hurdles

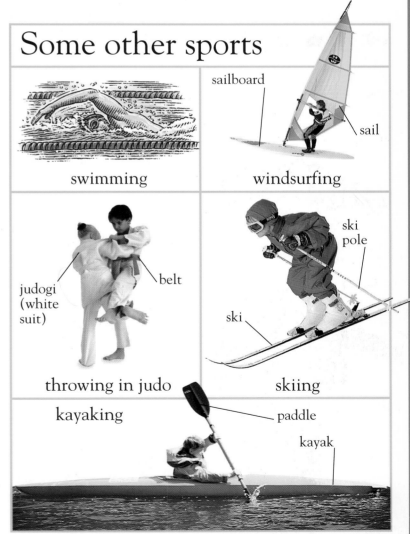

Some other sports

swimming

sailboard

sail

windsurfing

judogi (white suit)

belt

throwing in judo

ski pole

ski

skiing

kayaking

paddle

kayak

Where people live

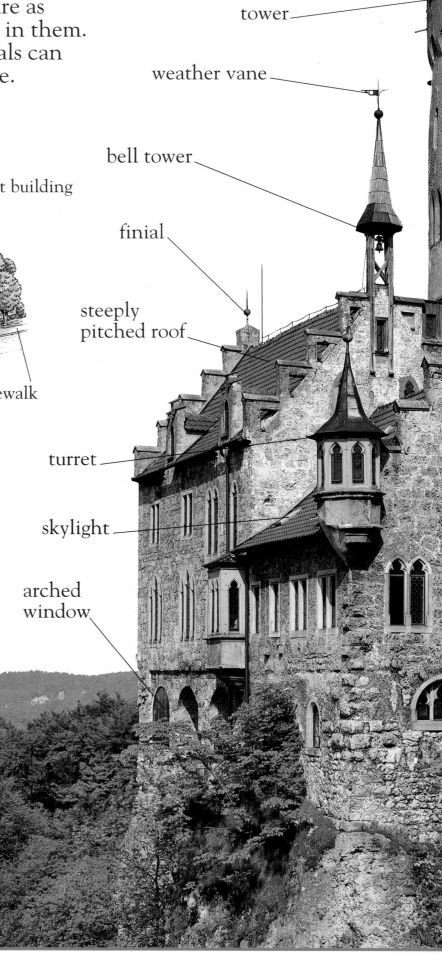

A stone castle

Everyone needs a place to call home, where they can feel safe, shelter from the weather, and store their possessions. Homes around the world are as different as the people and families that live in them. Usually they are built from whatever materials can be found locally – mud, wood, brick, or stone.

tower

weather vane

bell tower

finial

steeply pitched roof

turret

skylight

arched window

Life in the city suburbs

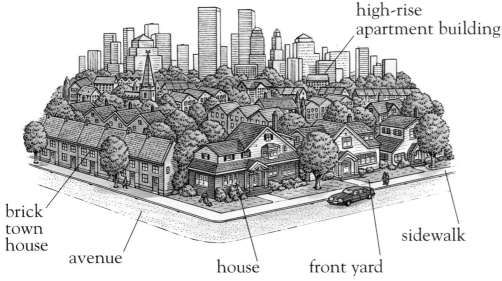

high-rise apartment building

brick town house

avenue

house

front yard

sidewalk

Homes built on water

pilothouse

chimney

cabin

a flat-bottomed houseboat barge

ladder

window

stilt support

wooden longhouses on stilts

battlements

Homes in the country

flat roof

a mobile home in Australia

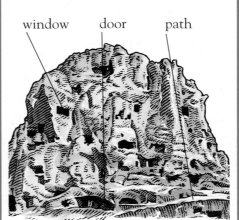
window   door   path

cave dwellings in Turkey

guyline   fabric roof

a Bedouin tent in the desert

stitched skin tent   guyline

a yurt in Mongolia

thatched roof   mud wall

Ethiopian thatched huts

balcony   sloping roof

a chalet in Switzerland

gatehouse

Homes in the town

window   roof eaves

an apartment tower

television antenna   shingled roof   entry

a ranch house

a house with a courtyard

21

Towns and cities

Cities and towns are busy places with streets of houses and other buildings where many people live, shop, and work together. These large communities often provide public services for the inhabitants, such as a police force, a fire service, hospitals, and libraries.

A city scene

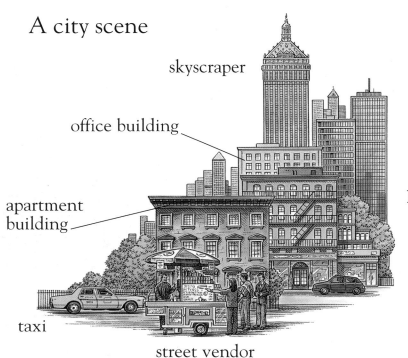

skyscraper

office building

apartment building

taxi

street vendor

A city square

streetlight

parking zone

street signs

one-way road system

fountain

Places of worship

minaret

a mosque

bell tower

a cathedral

domed roof

a synagogue

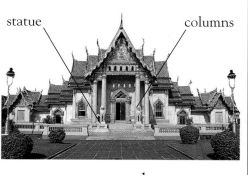

statue

columns

a temple

City services

fire trucks

a fire station

city skyline

entrance to
pedestrian mall

office building

City sights

awning

storefront

a busy street of stores

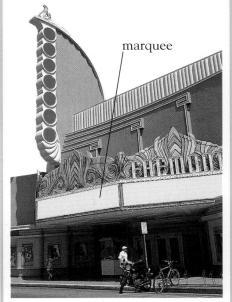

a grand hotel

marquee

glass exterior

an office building

a movie theater

gravel path

monument

flower bed

a city park

entrance to
subway system

café

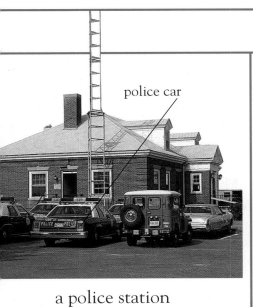

police car

a police station

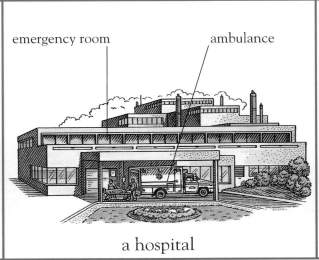

emergency room

ambulance

a hospital

reading room

a library

On the farm

Much of the countryside around the world is used as farmland to grow crops and to rear animals. Farms produce food all year round, as well as materials such as wool and rubber. Although some farms are large mechanized industries, many remain small and are run by families in traditional ways.

A dairy farm

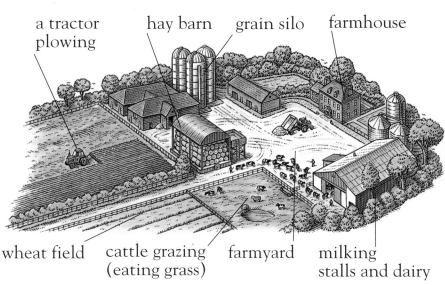

a tractor plowing

hay barn

grain silo

farmhouse

wheat field

cattle grazing (eating grass)

farmyard

milking stalls and dairy

Harvesting crops

tea bushes

rubber tree

picking tea leaves

combine harvester

harvesting wheat

tapping rubber

A tractor working the land

tractor driver

cab

exhaust pipe

engine

tire

power harrow

hub

Farm animals

herdsman

calf

a herd of cattle lowing

pannier

a donkey braying

woolly coat

a llama snorting

gosling

a gaggle of geese honking

nanny goat   horns

beard

kid

two goats bleating

comb

wattle

a rooster crowing

sheep dip   farmhand

sheepdog

a flock of sheep bleating

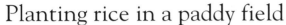

Planting rice in a paddy field

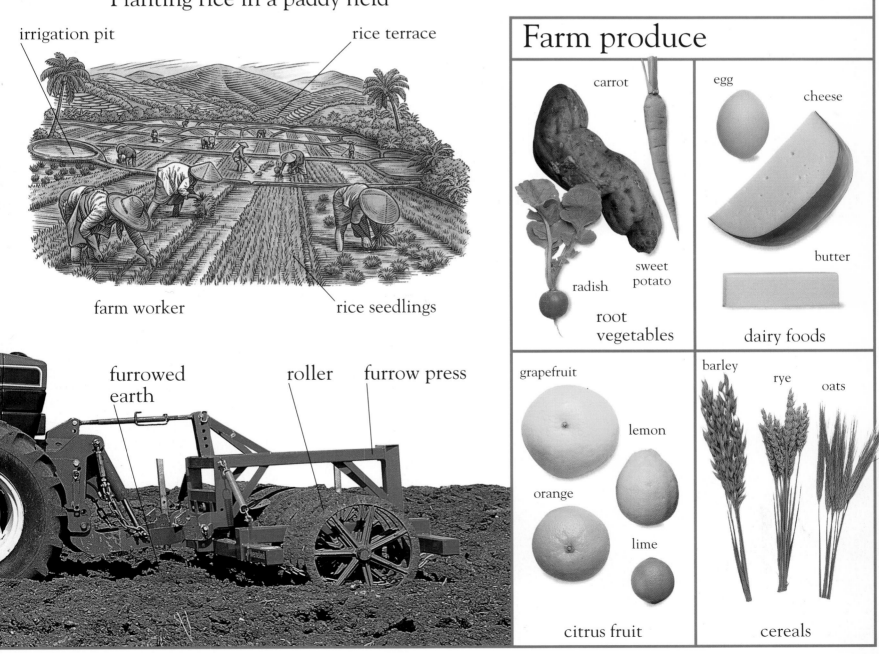

irrigation pit

rice terrace

farm worker

rice seedlings

furrowed earth

roller

furrow press

Farm produce

carrot

egg   cheese

butter

radish   sweet potato

root vegetables

dairy foods

grapefruit

lemon

orange

lime

citrus fruit

barley   rye   oats

cereals

Traveling by road

M any different types of vehicles carry people and things from place to place. Some vehicles are pulled by animals or people, while others have engines, which run on gasoline or diesel fuel. All road transportation vehicles travel on wheels.

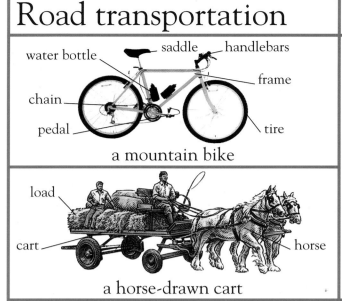

Road transportation

water bottle — saddle — handlebars
chain — frame
pedal — tire

a mountain bike

load — cart — horse

a horse-drawn cart

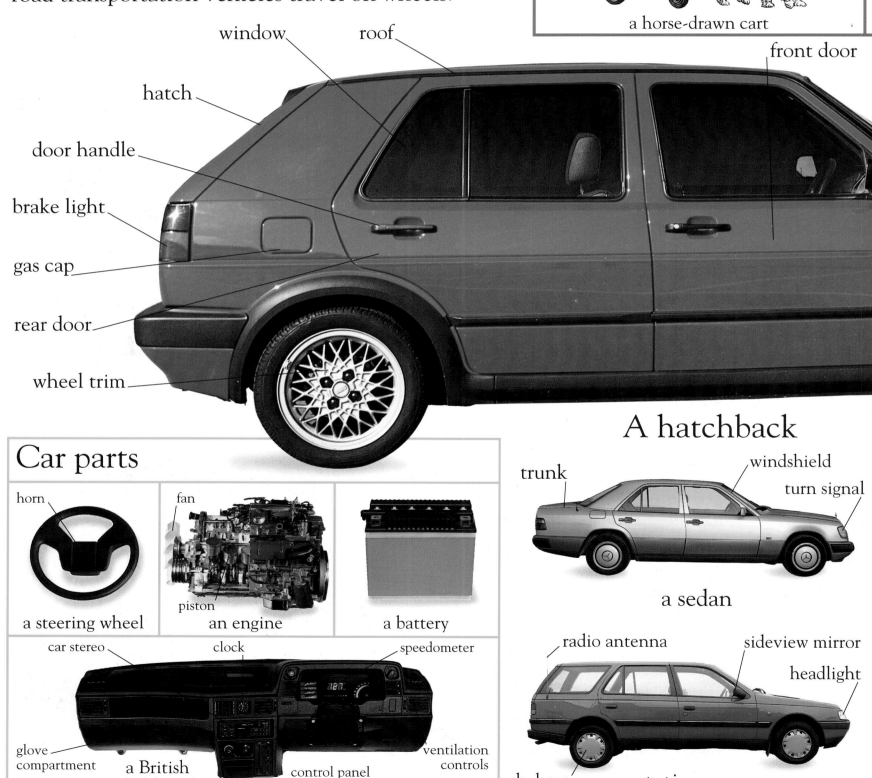

window — roof
hatch
door handle
brake light
gas cap
rear door
wheel trim

front door

Car parts

horn

a steering wheel

fan
piston

an engine

a battery

car stereo — clock — speedometer
glove compartment
a British dashboard
control panel
ventilation controls

A hatchback

trunk — windshield — turn signal

a sedan

radio antenna — sideview mirror — headlight
hubcap
a station wagon

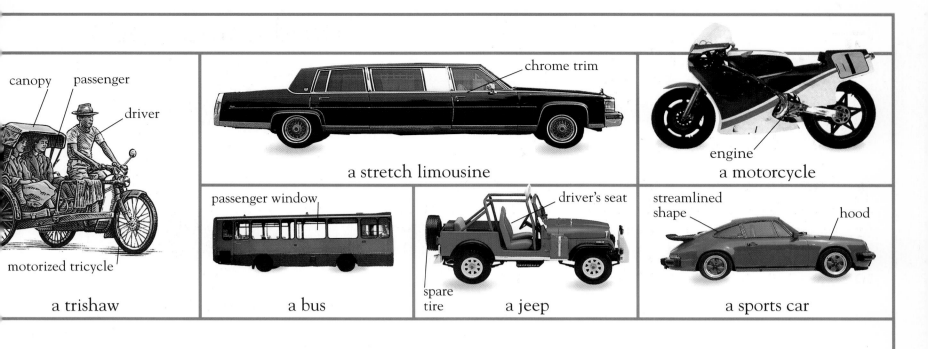

canopy   passenger

driver

motorized tricycle

a trishaw

chrome trim

a stretch limousine

engine

a motorcycle

passenger window

a bus

driver's seat

spare tire

a jeep

streamlined shape

hood

a sports car

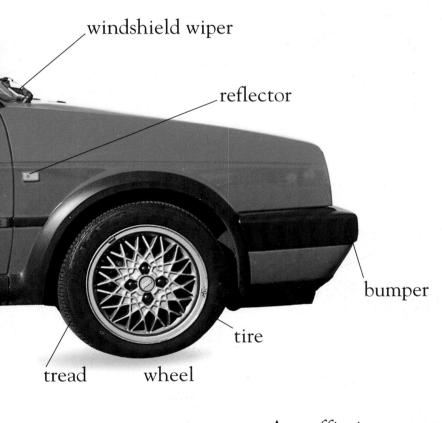

windshield wiper

reflector

bumper

tire

tread   wheel

A variety of working vehicles

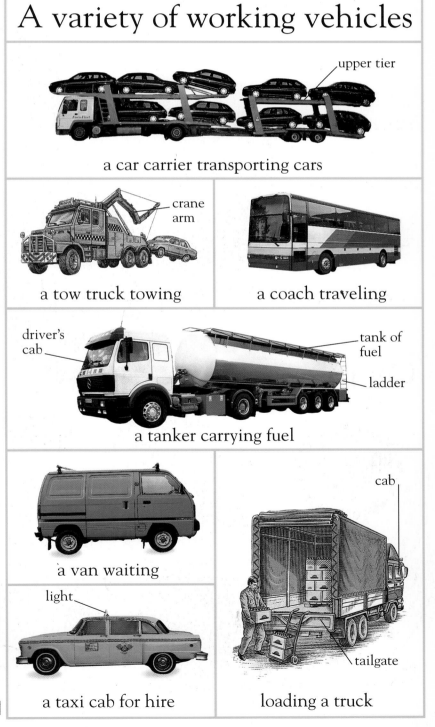

upper tier

a car carrier transporting cars

crane arm

a tow truck towing

a coach traveling

driver's cab

tank of fuel

ladder

a tanker carrying fuel

a van waiting

light

a taxi cab for hire

cab

tailgate

loading a truck

A traffic jam

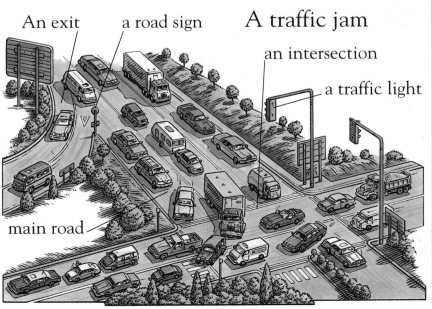

An exit   a road sign

an intersection

a traffic light

main road

Traveling by rail

Large numbers of people use trains to travel quickly from place to place. Trains are also used to carry heavy loads. For many years, trains ran on steam, produced by coal burning in their engines. Nowadays, many trains run on diesel fuel or electric power, which runs either through electrified tracks or through overhead wires.

signal   ticket office   waiting room

schedule

ticket inspector

railroad track

platform

porter

luggage

At a railroad station

all-around windows

Inside an observation car

driver's cab   horn

windshield   ladder   insignia

headlight

fender

A variety of trains

an electric train speeding

windshield wiper

a diesel train engine

headlight   chimney   coal supply

a steam locomotive engine

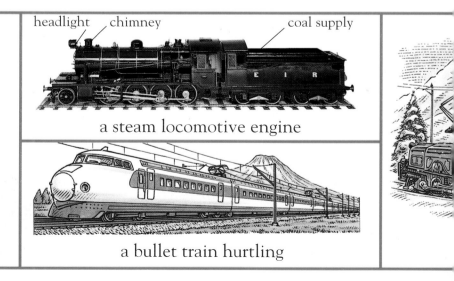

a bullet train hurtling

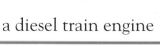

Urban trains

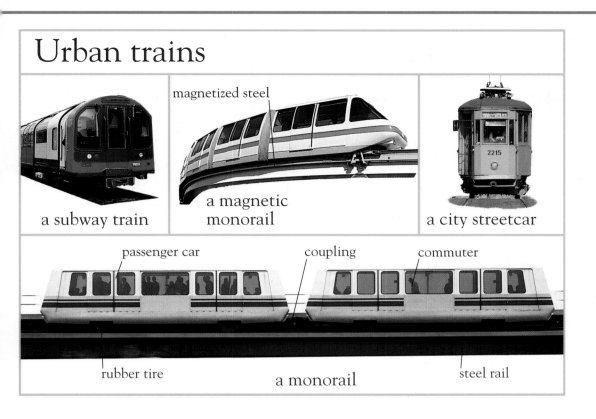

magnetized steel

a subway train

a magnetic monorail

a city streetcar

passenger car   coupling   commuter

rubber tire   a monorail   steel rail

Working trains

buffer

a shunter

tanker car   boxcar

a cargo train

crane

a breakdown train

gantry

loading a freight car

observation car

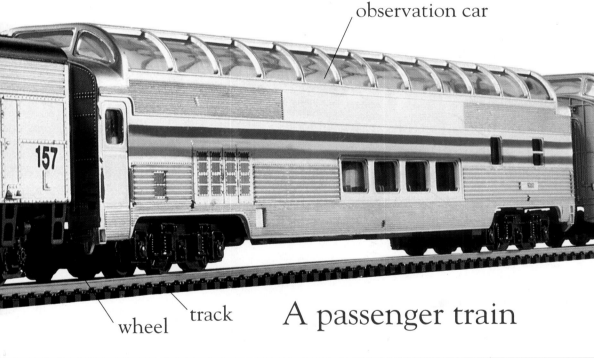

157

wheel   track   A passenger train

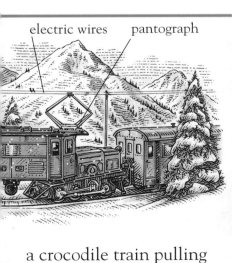

electric wires   pantograph

a crocodile train pulling

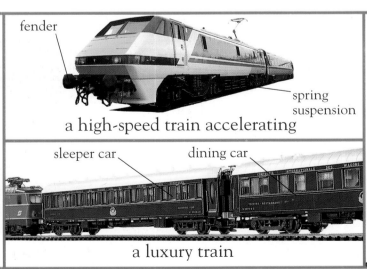

fender

spring suspension

a high-speed train accelerating

sleeper car   dining car

a luxury train

a rack-and-pinion train climbing

angled windows

Traveling by sea

All sorts of ships and boats travel on the sea. Some have sails and are driven by wind power, while others have engines and carry cargo and passengers over long distances. Boats unload their cargo in a port or harbor, a sheltered place on a coast where they can drop anchor safely.

Ship's equipment

a sextant

a steering wheel

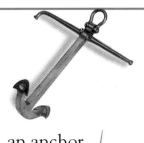

an anchor

rope

a life buoy

The harbor

lighthouse harbor wall lifeboat station crane warehouse quay

slipway

Ocean liner

porthole

radar mast

lifeboat

bridge

PACIFIC PRINCESS

bow

PACIFIC PRINCESS

anchor

hull

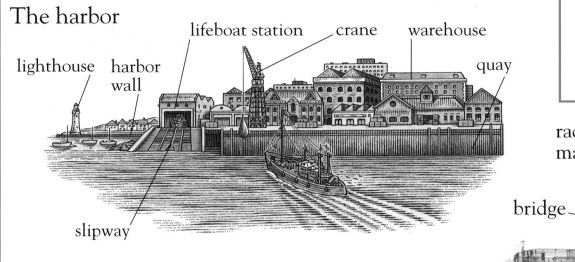

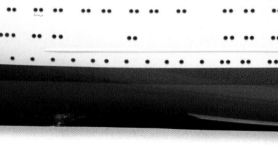

Ships and boats

gun turret helicopter pad

F209

a frigate patrolling

oar

outrigger

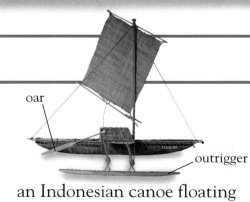

an Indonesian canoe floating

mainsail
spinnaker

a yacht heeling

container cargo

a container ship shipping

periscope

conning tower

a submarine diving

propeller

a hovercraft skimming

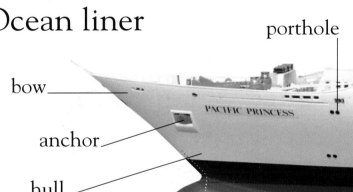

30

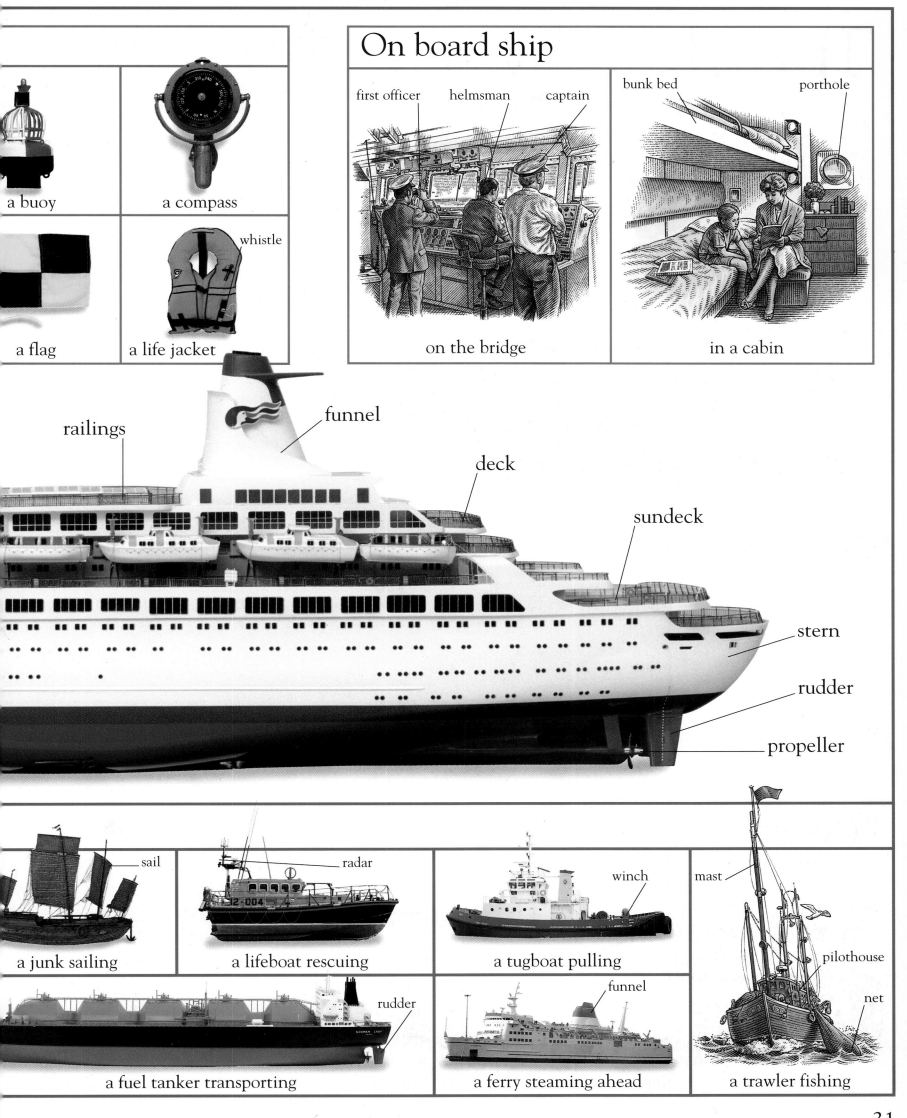

a buoy

a compass

a flag

a life jacket

whistle

On board ship

first officer   helmsman   captain

bunk bed   porthole

on the bridge

in a cabin

railings

funnel

deck

sundeck

stern

rudder

propeller

a junk sailing

sail

a lifeboat rescuing

radar

a tugboat pulling

winch

mast

pilothouse

net

a fuel tanker transporting

rudder

a ferry steaming ahead

funnel

a trawler fishing

Traveling by air

The Wright brothers flew the first airplane in 1903. Since then, flying has made it easy for people to travel long distances fast. There are many types of aircraft that people now fly for business and pleasure.

a stunt plane

colored smoke trail

An acrobatic air display team

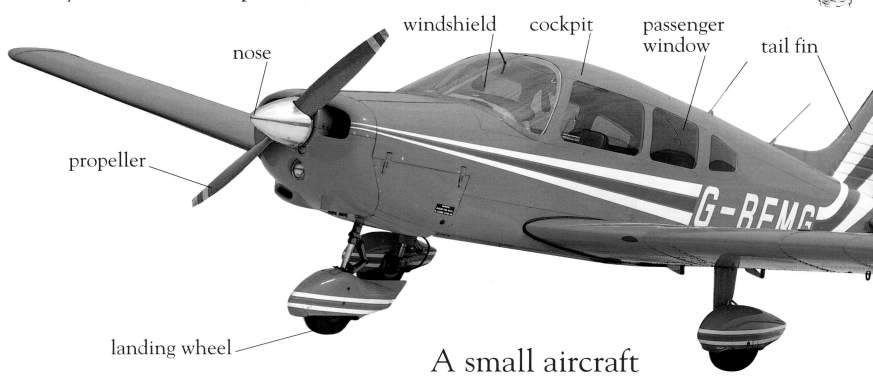

windshield
nose
cockpit
passenger window
tail fin
propeller
G-BEMG
landing wheel

A small aircraft

Passenger planes

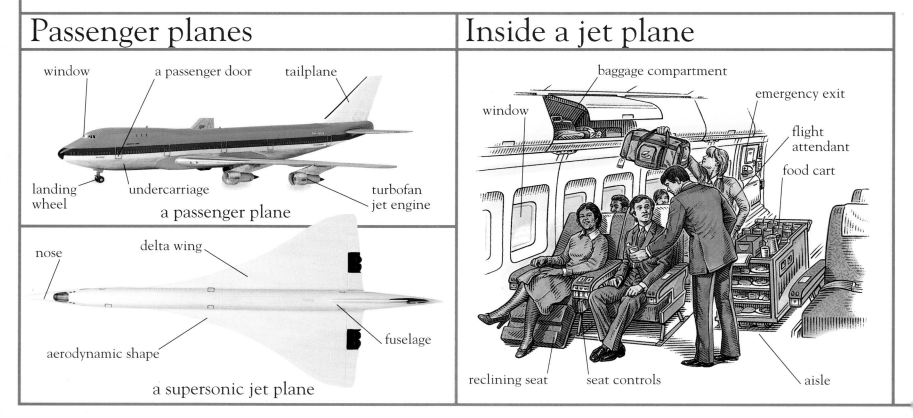

window
a passenger door
tailplane
landing wheel
undercarriage
turbofan jet engine

a passenger plane

nose
delta wing
aerodynamic shape
fuselage

a supersonic jet plane

Inside a jet plane

baggage compartment
emergency exit
window
flight attendant
food cart
reclining seat
seat controls
aisle

Flying for fun

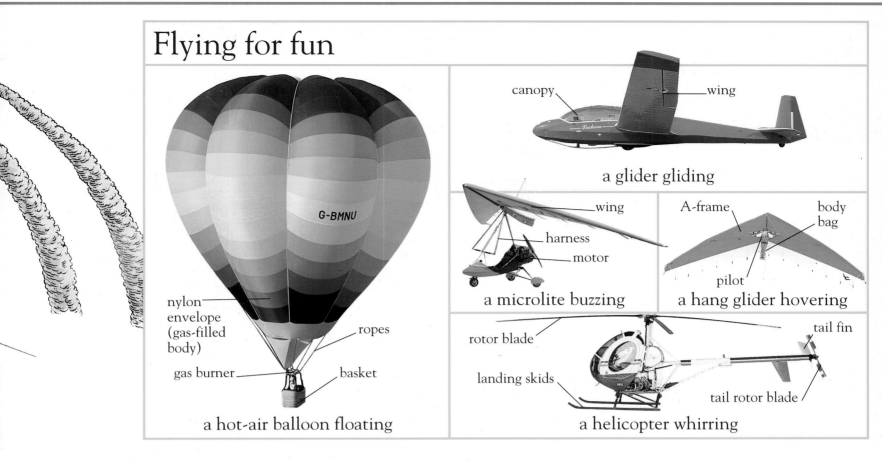

a glider gliding

canopy · wing

a microlite buzzing

wing · harness · motor

a hang glider hovering

A-frame · body bag · pilot

a hot-air balloon floating

nylon envelope (gas-filled body) · ropes · gas burner · basket

a helicopter whirring

rotor blade · landing skids · tail fin · tail rotor blade

Working planes

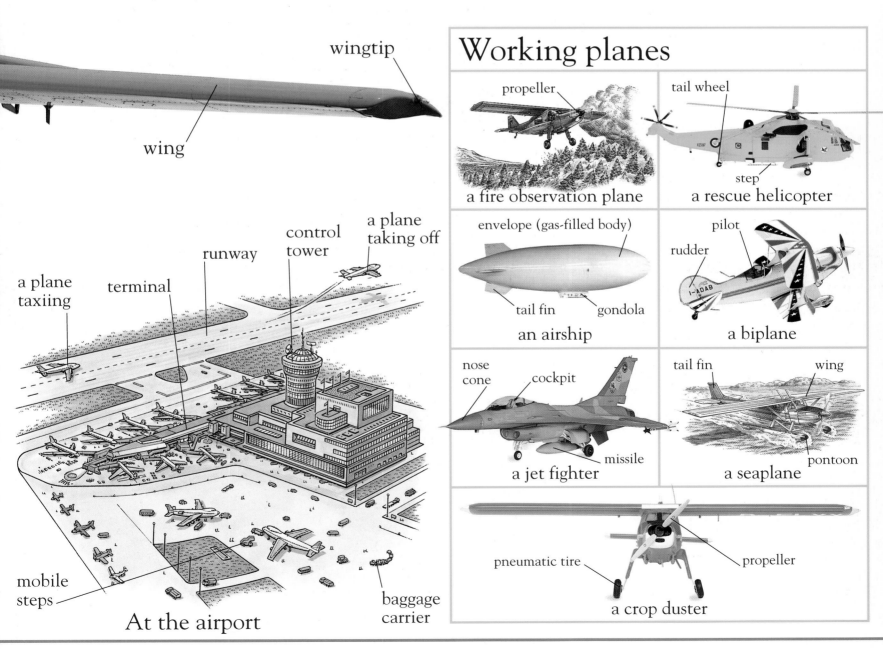

wingtip · wing

a fire observation plane

propeller

a rescue helicopter

tail wheel · step

an airship

envelope (gas-filled body) · tail fin · gondola

a biplane

pilot · rudder

a jet fighter

nose cone · cockpit · missile

a seaplane

tail fin · wing · pontoon

a crop duster

pneumatic tire · propeller

At the airport

wingtip · wing · a plane taking off · control tower · runway · terminal · a plane taxiing · mobile steps · baggage carrier

Mammals

Mammals are warm-blooded animals that give birth to live young. The parents look after their young and feed them on milk. Mammals are usually covered with hair or fur. They use lungs to breathe and are intelligent animals with large brains. Human beings are mammals.

A bat

finger

large ear

wing membrane

claw

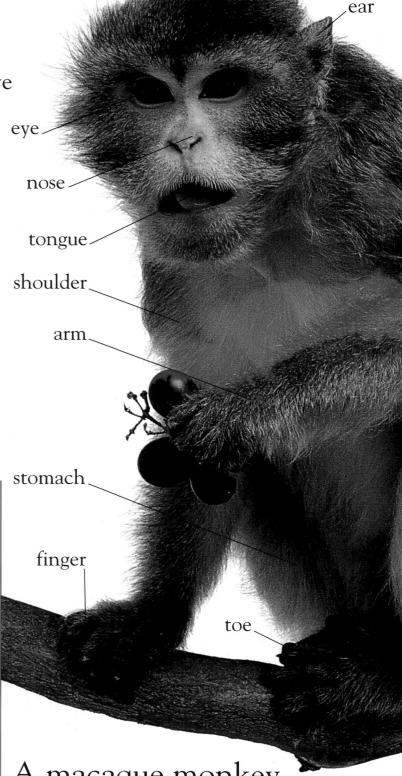

A macaque monkey

ear

eye

nose

tongue

shoulder

arm

stomach

finger

toe

Mammal heads

trunk

an elephant

tusk

snout

fangs

a fox

whiskers

a sea lion

a camel

muzzle

mane

forelock

nostril

a horse

flipper

beak

A school of dolphins

A pride of lions

mane

lioness

lion

cub

furry coat

leg

tail

Mammal coverings

striped fur for camouflage

a tiger stalking

spotted coat

hoof

a fawn trotting

three toes

shaggy hair

a sloth hanging

sharp quills

a porcupine scurrying

tough, leathery hide

horn

a rhinoceros chewing

mother giraffe

dappled skin

calf

scutes (armor plates)

bristles

an armadillo hunting

a giraffe calf suckling

Mammal homes

dried grass

feathers

branches

a squirrel in its drey

baby moles

nest

tunnel

a mole in its underground burrow

35

Reptiles

Reptiles are scaly-skinned, cold-blooded animals, such as snakes. Some reptiles live in water and some live on land. Most reptiles live in warm parts of the world. They use the warmth of the sun to give them energy to move. Young reptiles hatch from eggs.

camouflaged (hidden) brown skin

Gabon vipers hiding

A variety of reptiles

scaly skin

an eyed lizard

clubbed toes

green body for camouflage

a Madagascan gecko

leg

crest

a tuatara

beak

shell

leg

a starred tortoise

small front leg

large back foot

a basilisk lizard

strong jaws

spiky, ridged back

powerful tail

a Nile crocodile

swiveling eye

crest

A chameleon

ridged back

gripping feet

clasping toes

claw

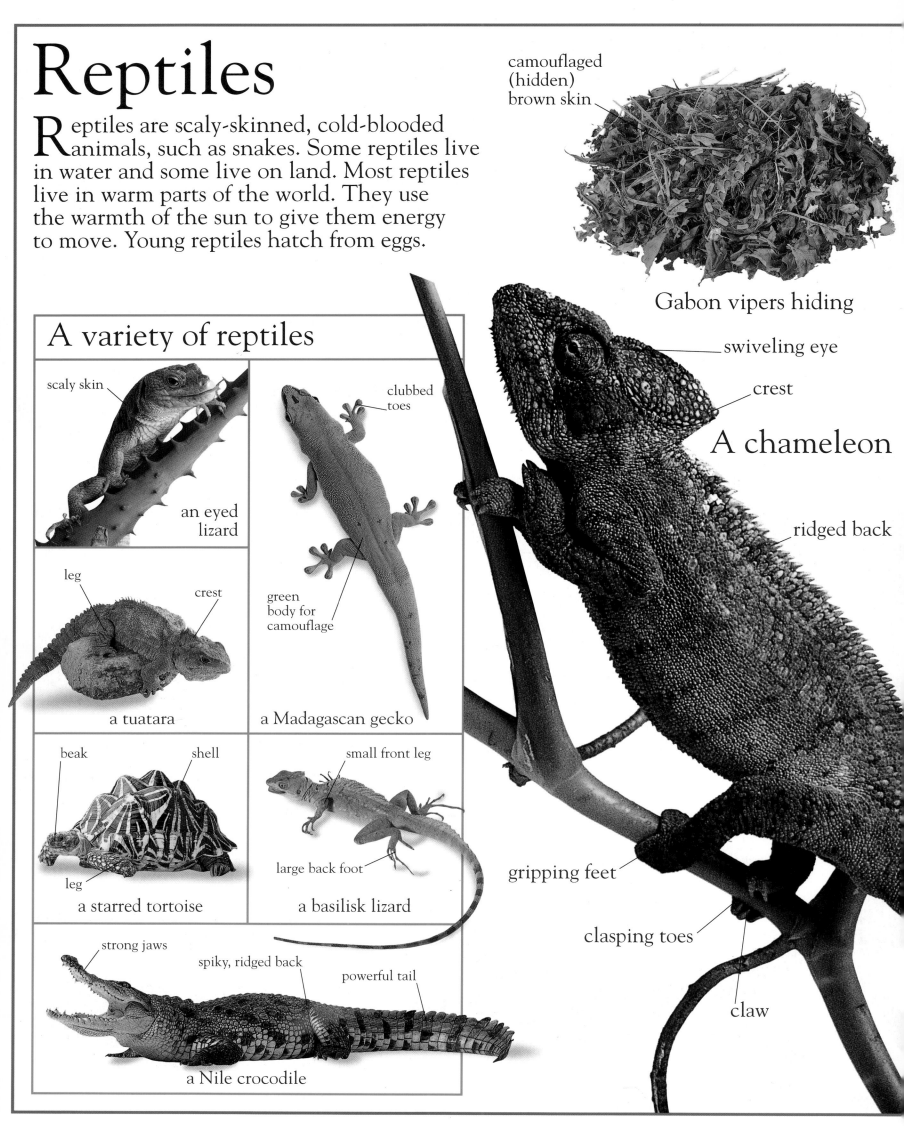

A leopard tortoise hatching

crack in eggshell
egg tooth
egg
baby tortoise

1 a tortoise chips a hole in its shell

eggshell
kicking leg

2 the tortoise struggles out of the egg

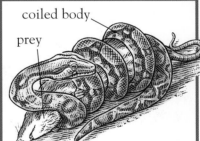

bony, plated shell for protection
head
clawed foot

3 the tortoise crawls away

an iguana basking in the sun

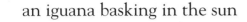

ridged spine

scaly skin

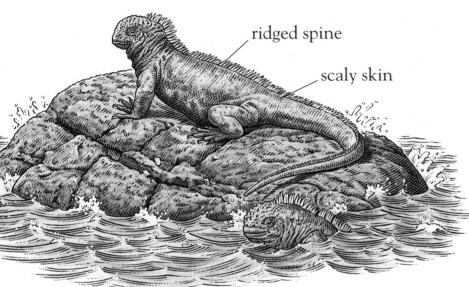

an iguana swimming

A pair of marine iguanas

scaly skin

prehensile tail for balance

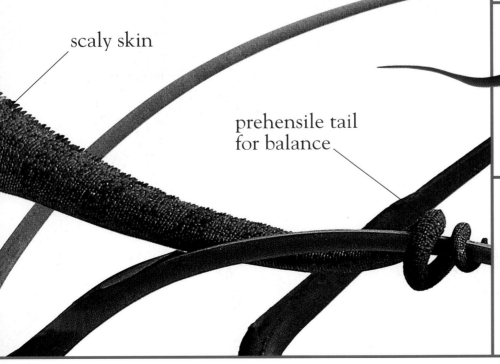

A variety of snakes

checkered markings

a corn snake writhing

scaly skin

beady eye

a milk snake slithering

tongue

a grass snake

coiled body
prey

a boa constrictor

extended hood

a cobra hissing

bright green body

a vine snake hunting

egg
wide-open jaws

an African egg-eating snake swallowing

Birds

Birds come in many shapes and sizes. All birds have wings, but not all of them can fly. Birds are the only animals that have feathers. They also have beaks and lay eggs.

A red-fronted parrot

nostril

head

eye

hooked beak

nape

breast

belly

leg

ankle

foot

toe

claw

Beaks

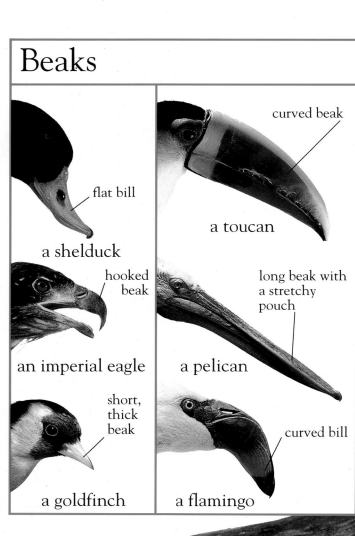

flat bill

a shelduck

curved beak

a toucan

hooked beak

an imperial eagle

long beak with a stretchy pouch

a pelican

short, thick beak

a goldfinch

curved bill

a flamingo

Growing up

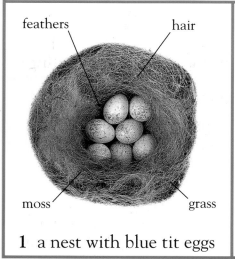

feathers

hair

moss

grass

1 a nest with blue tit eggs

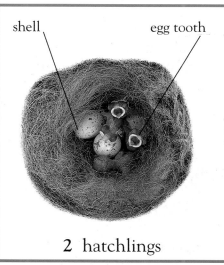

shell

egg tooth

2 hatchlings

feather tufts

3 young nestlings

feathers

4 fledglings

Macaw feathers

shaft

soft down feathers

barb

quill

a flight feather

body feathers

wing

tail

A variety of birds

wing feather

talons

an owl swooping

sharp beak

a kiwi hunting

beak

claws

tail

lorikeets preening

comb

egg

a hen nesting

nectar-drinking beak

a hummingbird hovering

a Japanese grosbeak finch perching

long neck

knee

webbed foot

a flamingo wading

a skein of geese migrating

flipper

waterproof feathers

iceberg

A group of penguins

a blue pigeon flying

fantail

fanned tail

a peacock displaying

Sea creatures

Many different creatures live in the seas and oceans of the world. Most sea creatures breathe through gills, although some fish have lungs. Fish are the largest group of animals that live in the salty waters of the sea. Many other creatures live on the seabed, on rocks, and on the seashore.

A shoal of flying fish

"wing" fin
for gliding

Some types of fish

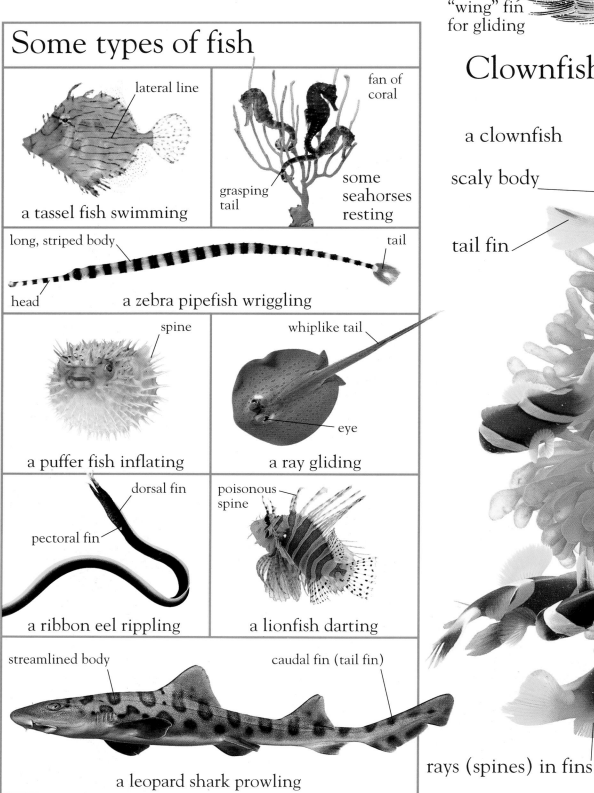

lateral line

a tassel fish swimming

fan of coral

grasping tail

some seahorses resting

long, striped body

tail

head

a zebra pipefish wriggling

spine

a puffer fish inflating

whiplike tail

eye

a ray gliding

dorsal fin

pectoral fin

a ribbon eel rippling

poisonous spine

a lionfish darting

streamlined body

caudal fin (tail fin)

a leopard shark prowling

Clownfish and anemones

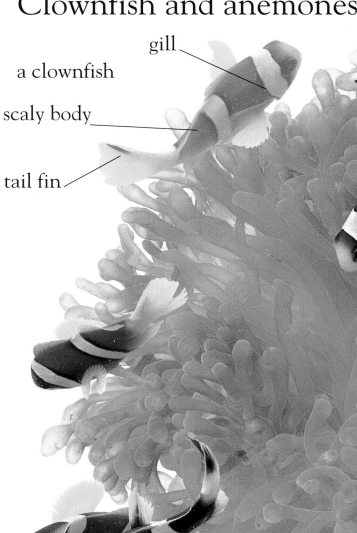

gill

a clownfish

scaly body

tail fin

rays (spines) in fins

Mollusks (soft-bodied creatures)

a barnacle — a whelk shell

antenna

a hermit crab

encrusted shell

mussels on a rock

siphon (waste tube)

a big blue clam

claw

exoskeleton (outer shell)

an edible crab

a lettuce slug

mouth

frilly edge

sucker

tentacle

an octopus

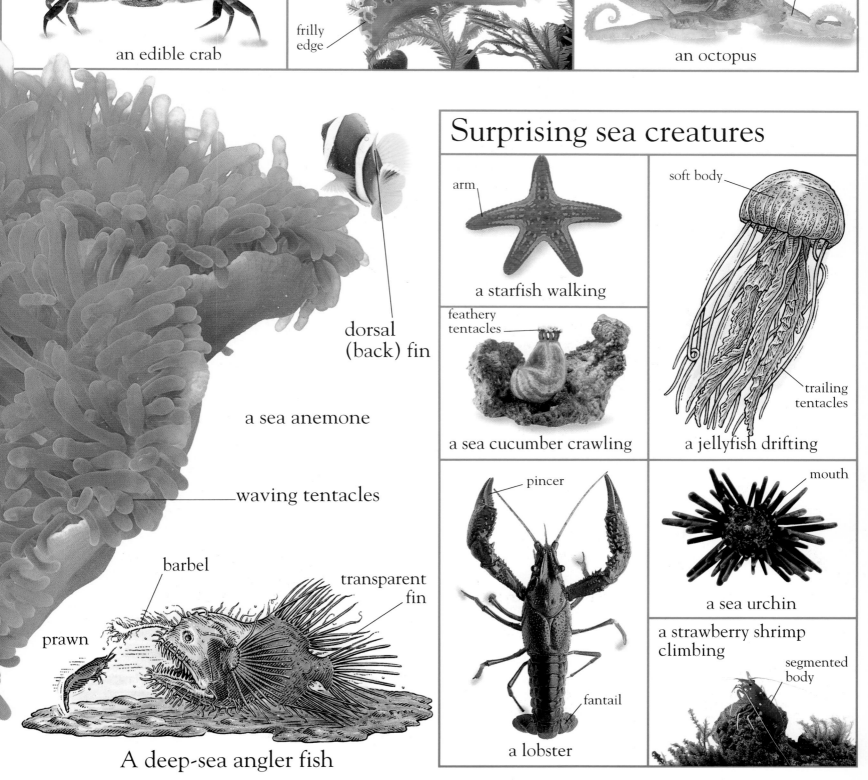

dorsal (back) fin

a sea anemone

waving tentacles

barbel

prawn

transparent fin

A deep-sea angler fish

Surprising sea creatures

arm

a starfish walking

feathery tentacles

a sea cucumber crawling

soft body

trailing tentacles

a jellyfish drifting

pincer

fantail

a lobster

mouth

a sea urchin

a strawberry shrimp climbing

segmented body

Swamp and river life

Many different creatures build their homes in or near swamps and rivers. Most of these animals can swim and catch food in the water. Many plants also grow on riverbanks and in muddy swamp waters.

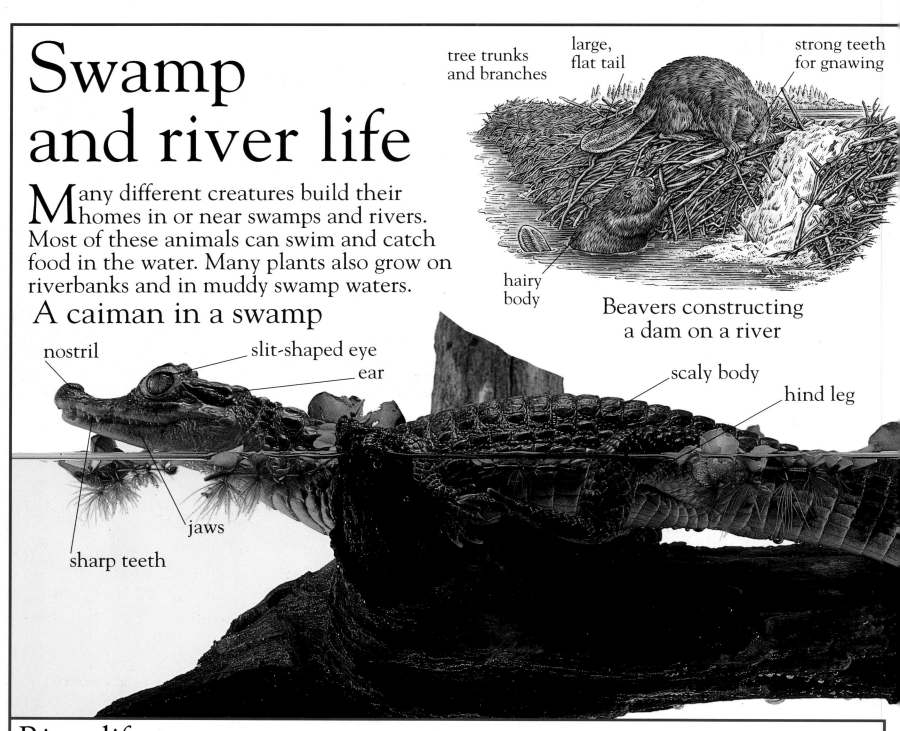

Beavers constructing a dam on a river

tree trunks and branches

large, flat tail

strong teeth for gnawing

hairy body

A caiman in a swamp

nostril

slit-shaped eye

ear

jaws

sharp teeth

scaly body

hind leg

River life

river plants swaying

yellow flag iris

water arum

a brown rat diving

ear

a crayfish swimming

segmented body

tail

antenna

swimmeret (leg for swimming)

a night-heron perching

beak

a pink-eared duck standing

breast

a mayfly clinging

long, jointed leg

large front wing

small back wing

tails for balance

Swamp life

piranha fish swimming

a water hyacinth blooming

a mudskipper resting
leglike fin — gill cover

an orb weaver spider scuttling
orchid

a purple gallinule walking
spreading toes — long leg

waxy, waterproof petal

a mangrove snake lurking
forked tongue

two fiddler crabs fighting
giant pincer — eye on stalk

The life cycle of a trout

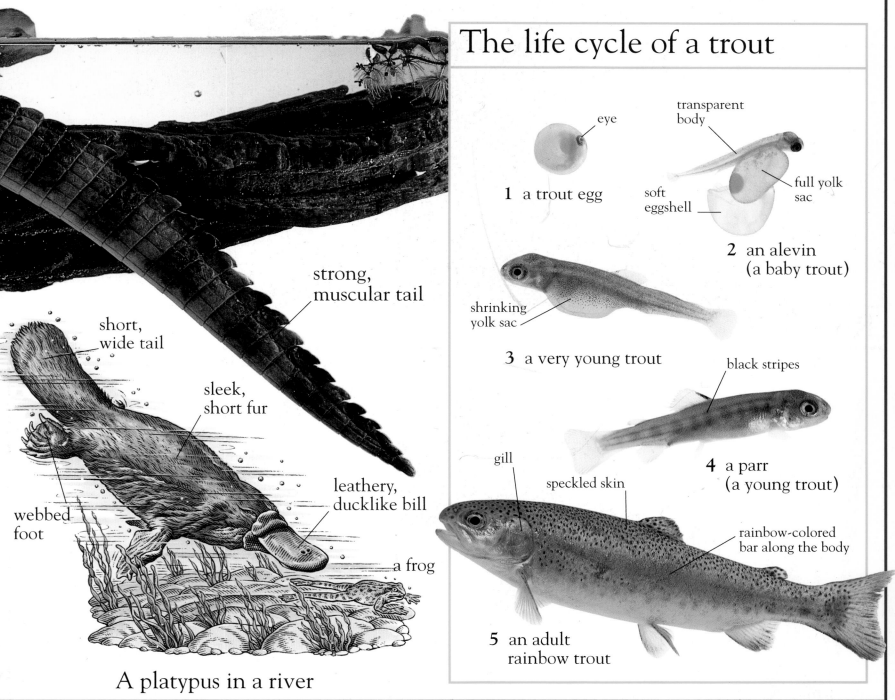

strong, muscular tail

short, wide tail

sleek, short fur

leathery, ducklike bill

webbed foot

a frog

A platypus in a river

1 a trout egg
eye

transparent body

2 an alevin (a baby trout)
soft eggshell — full yolk sac

3 a very young trout
shrinking yolk sac

4 a parr (a young trout)
black stripes

5 an adult rainbow trout
gill
speckled skin
rainbow-colored bar along the body

Amphibians

All amphibians start their lives in water. Later, when they become adults, they leave the water to live on land, except for newts. All amphibians breathe through gills when they are young. However, most adult amphibians use lungs for breathing.

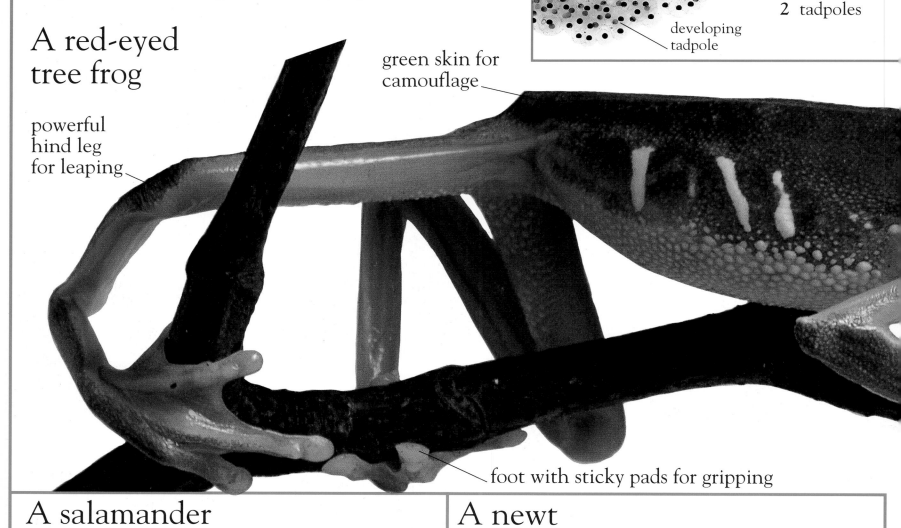

The life cycle of a frog

1 frog spawn (eggs)

jelly

developing tadpole

wriggling tail

2 tadpoles

A red-eyed tree frog

powerful hind leg for leaping

green skin for camouflage

foot with sticky pads for gripping

A salamander

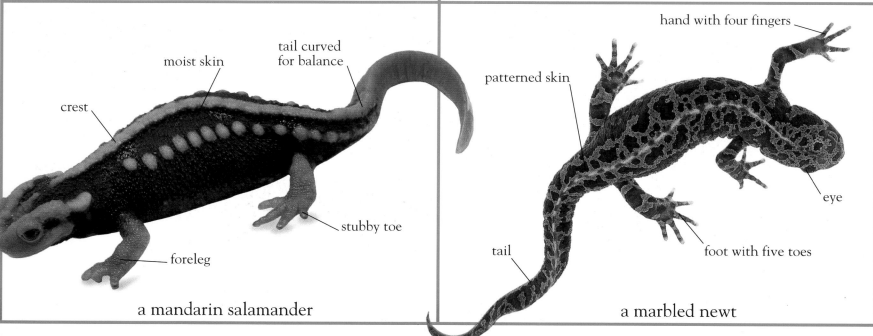

crest

moist skin

tail curved for balance

stubby toe

foreleg

a mandarin salamander

A newt

hand with four fingers

patterned skin

eye

tail

foot with five toes

a marbled newt

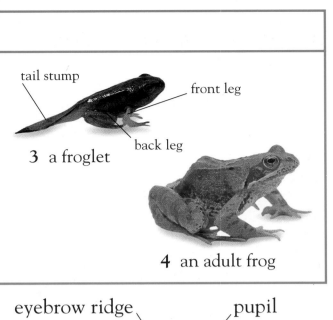

tail stump

front leg

back leg

3 a froglet

4 an adult frog

eyebrow ridge

pupil

nostril

mouth

foreleg

long finger

feathery gills

tiny eyes

albino (white) skin

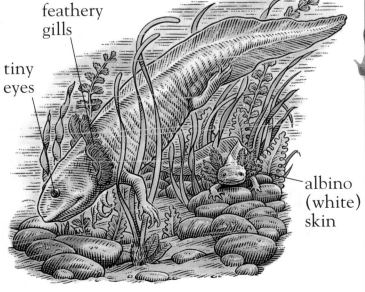

An axolotl

A variety of amphibians

stretched-out body and legs

a damselfly

a European common frog leaping

flicking tongue

eggs

a midwife toad brooding spawn

wide mouth

tree frogs climbing

warning color

a poison-dart frog sitting

horns over eyes

warty skin

a horned toad squatting

water plant

webbed foot

a European common frog

damp skin

tomato frogs clustering

throat pouch

lily pad

a bullfrog croaking

bulging eyes

glistening skin

yellow patches

a fire salamander creeping

Mini-beasts

Most mini-beasts belong to a group of animals called invertebrates. These animals do not have a backbone. Instead, they have a hard, outer skin that is shed often as the animal grows. Most mini-beasts hatch out of eggs. Many of them can fly, and some live in large colonies, or groups.

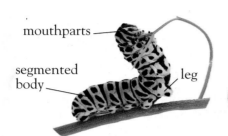

thorax
(upper body)

antenna

head

eye

abdomen
(lower body)

The life cycle of a butterfly

egg

plant
stalk

1 a ripe egg

mouthparts

segmented
body

leg

2 a caterpillar (larva)

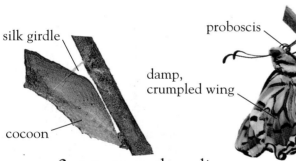

silk girdle

cocoon

3 a pupa or chrysalis

proboscis

damp,
crumpled wing

empty
cocoon

4 an adult butterfly

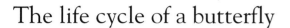

Different mini-beasts

a scorpion scurrying

pincer   stinger

furry legs

a tarantula crawling

a millipede wriggling

antenna

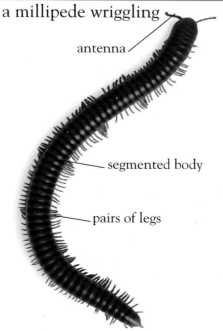

segmented body

pairs of legs

transparent
wing

blood
vein

a dragonfly hovering

wing case

a ladybug scuttling

wing

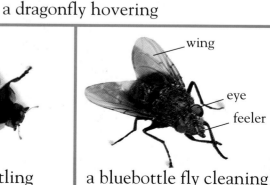

eye

feeler

a bluebottle fly cleaning

46

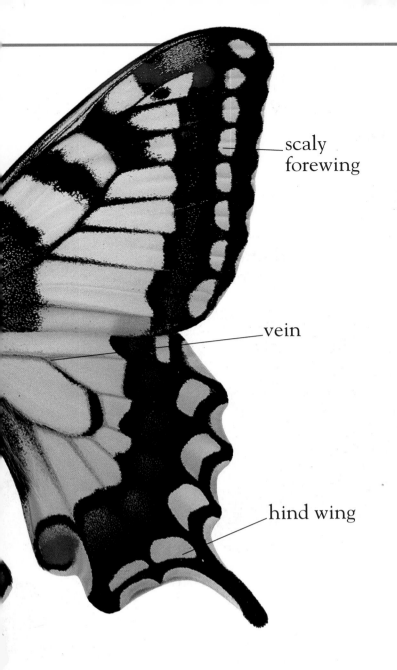

scaly forewing

vein

hind wing

A line of leaf-cutting ants

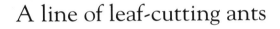

Mini-beast homes

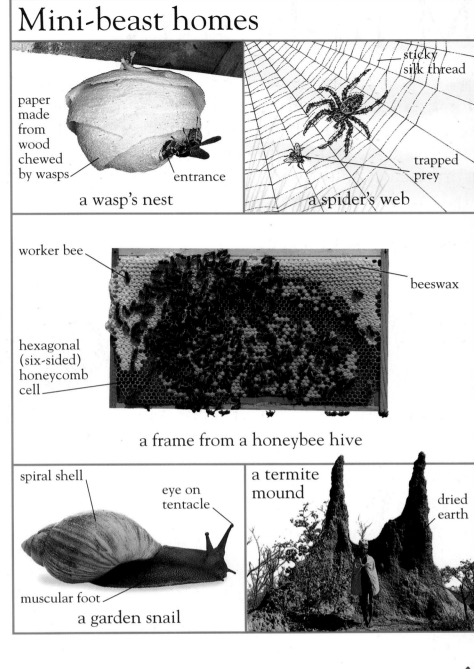

paper made from wood chewed by wasps

entrance

a wasp's nest

sticky silk thread

trapped prey

a spider's web

worker bee

beeswax

hexagonal (six-sided) honeycomb cell

a frame from a honeybee hive

spiral shell

eye on tentacle

muscular foot

a garden snail

a termite mound

dried earth

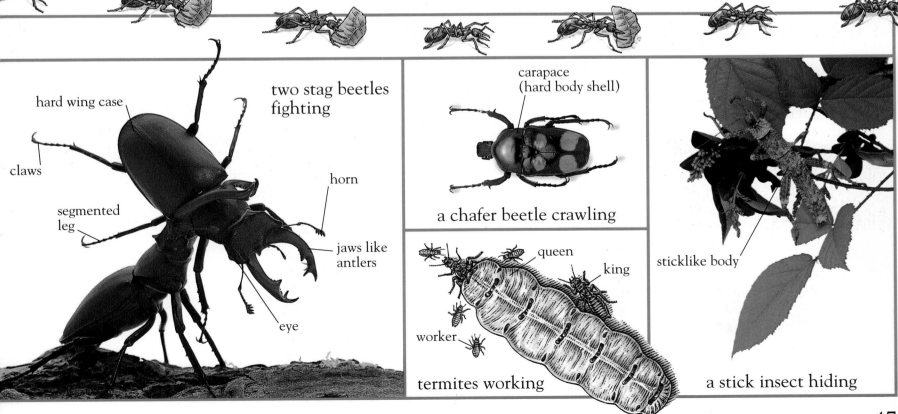

two stag beetles fighting

hard wing case

claws

segmented leg

horn

jaws like antlers

eye

carapace (hard body shell)

a chafer beetle crawling

sticklike body

queen

king

worker

termites working

a stick insect hiding

Plants

Different types of plants grow in hot, cold, wet, or dry places. Some plants are tiny, while others grow huge, such as trees. Many plants have flowers, which produce seeds to make new plants. Most plants need light, water, and air to grow well.

A variety of plants

prickly flower head

small flowers

spiky leaf

a thistle flower

spine

a Ferocactus

flower

seeds

seed pod

a poppy flower

A hibiscus flower

stigma

stamen

pollen

petal

calyx

stalk

flower bud

flower head

veins

A Venus's fly-trap

trigger hairs

teeth

trap

leaf stalk

leaf

stem

midrib

trapped insect

frond

rhizome

root

a fern

a sunflower

ray florets

disk florets (flowers)

flower

thick, shiny leaf

bulb

roots

a tulip bulb in bloom

tiny seed

a dandelion head

a bee pollinating a rose

pollen sac on leg

bee sipping nectar

leaf

stem

tuber

root

a potato plant

flower

tough, waxy leaf

a waterlily

A beech tree germinating (growing from seed)

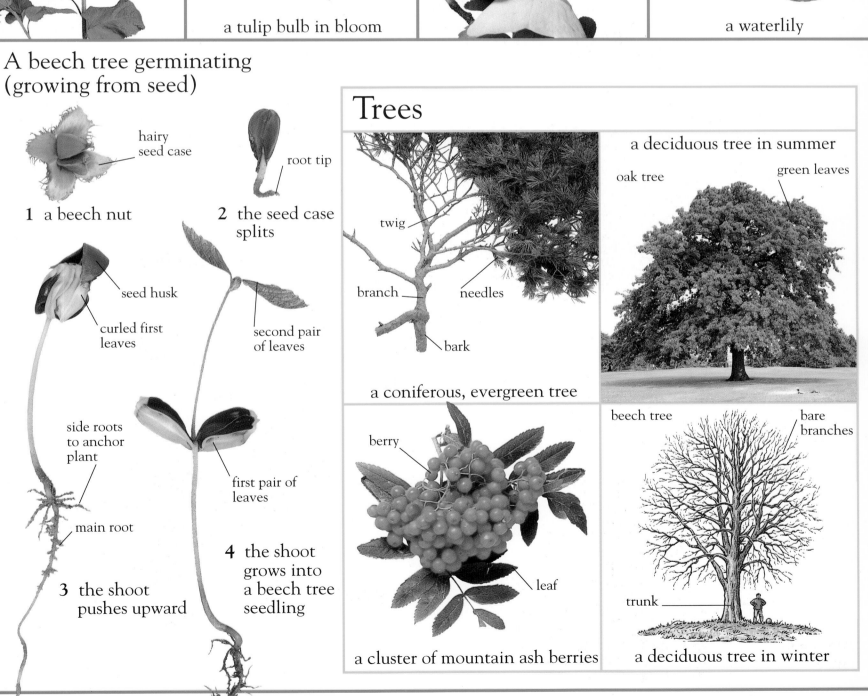

hairy seed case

1 a beech nut

root tip

2 the seed case splits

seed husk

curled first leaves

second pair of leaves

side roots to anchor plant

main root

first pair of leaves

3 the shoot pushes upward

4 the shoot grows into a beech tree seedling

Trees

twig

branch

needles

bark

a coniferous, evergreen tree

a deciduous tree in summer

oak tree

green leaves

berry

leaf

a cluster of mountain ash berries

beech tree

bare branches

trunk

a deciduous tree in winter

Land environments

Changes on the Earth over millions of years have created different landscapes and environments around the world. Some valleys were formed by glaciers during the Ice Ages. Some mountain ranges were formed when sections of the Earth's surface collided. Many unique types of plants and animals have developed to live in each kind of environment.

volcanic crater
peak
mountainside

In the mountains

On the plains

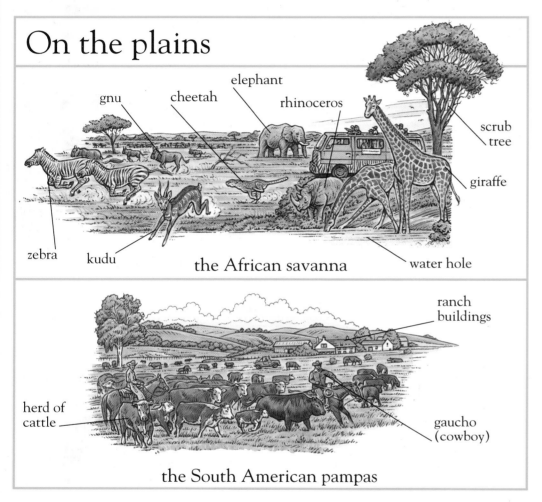

gnu
cheetah
elephant
rhinoceros
scrub tree
giraffe
zebra
kudu
water hole

the African savanna

ranch buildings
herd of cattle
gaucho (cowboy)

the South American pampas

Natural disasters

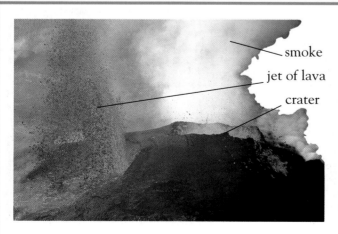

smoke
jet of lava
crater

a volcano erupting

cracked building
fissure in the ground

after an earthquake

mountaintop
snow line
slope
overhang
village

A mountain valley

waterfall

cliff

mountain ledge

forest

Forest and woodland

tall tree trunk

a redwood forest

a conifer tree farm

rough scrubland

canopy

a tropical rain forest

a broad-leaved forest

Desert places

sand dune

palm tree

a desert oasis

rock formation

a rocky desert

dune

camel trail

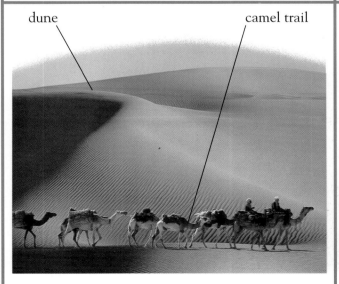
a sandy desert

cactus

an arid desert

Water environments

Much of the Earth is covered by water in the form of rivers, lakes, seas, and oceans. Over many years, the water and weather combine to form special environments and landscape features such as valleys, cliffs, and caves.

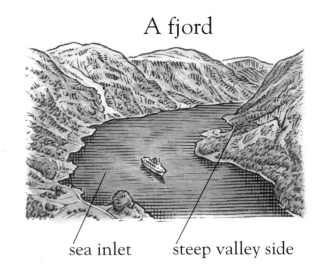

A fjord

sea inlet — steep valley side

Cold places

block of ice

an iceberg floating in the ocean

river of ice

a glacier in a mountain range

snow

a mountain avalanche

icicles on the seashore

reindeer — lichen

the frozen tundra

The coast

path   beach   rock   cave

rock strata (layers)   surf

Water sources

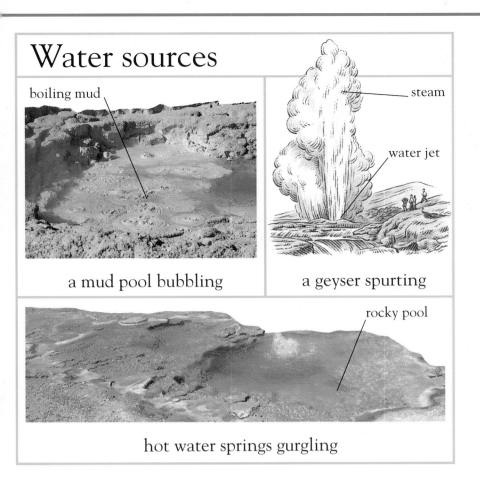

boiling mud

a mud pool bubbling

steam

water jet

a geyser spurting

rocky pool

hot water springs gurgling

wave

rock stack

sea

cliff top

Rivers and lakes

a river meandering through a rain forest

rock

white water

inflatable dinghy

river rapids raging

reflection of mountains

a still lake

torrent

a cascading waterfall

dam

a reservoir of water

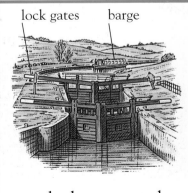

lock gates

barge

a lock on a canal

Weather

Our world, the Earth, is surrounded by a thick blanket of gases called the atmosphere. The lowest layer of the atmosphere is constantly swirling, and this creates the different forms of our weather – from warm, sunny days to raging thunderstorms and hurricanes.

Some types of weather

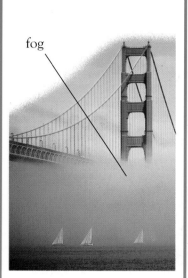
fog

a dull, foggy morning

lightning

a wild thunderstorm

a freezing cold day

a blustery, windy day

mist

a damp, rainy day

blue sky

a hot, sunny day

Landscape after a thunderstorm

bright sunlight

horizon

Forecasting the weather

Centigrade scale
Fahrenheit scale

temperature gauge
a thermometer

air pressure record
needle

a barograph

a weather satellite

warm front   cold front

isobar
a weather chart

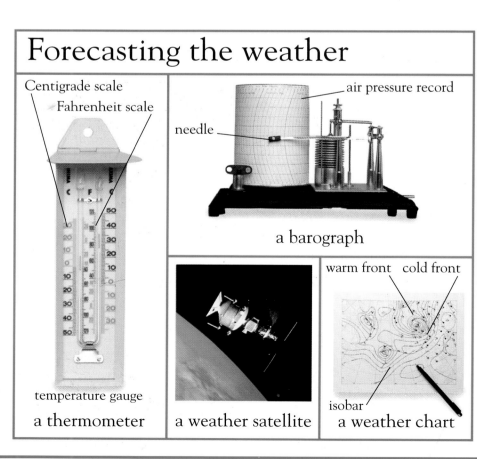

rainbow

storm clouds

blue sky

Different types of clouds

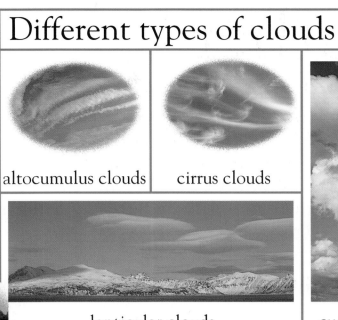

altocumulus clouds

cirrus clouds

lenticular clouds

cumulus clouds

A weather station

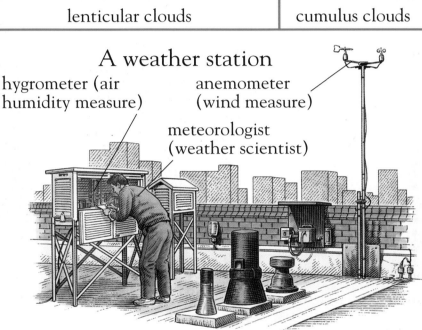

hygrometer (air humidity measure)

anemometer (wind measure)

meteorologist (weather scientist)

Extremes of weather

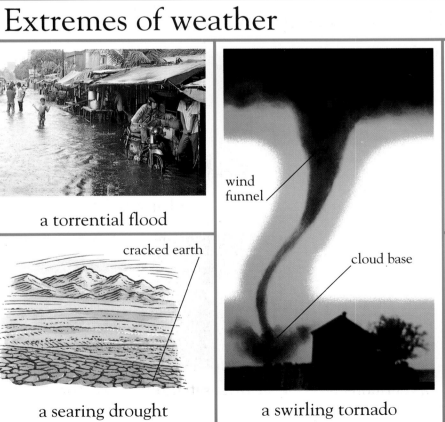

a torrential flood

wind funnel

cloud base

a swirling tornado

tidal wave

a violent hurricane

cracked earth

a searing drought

snowdrift

aftermath of a blizzard

a raging dust storm

Early life on Earth

The first plants and animals lived on the Earth more than 700 million years ago. Since then, many species have developed and then died out, continuously evolving. Dinosaurs lived on the Earth for about 165 million years, but became extinct (died out) long before the first humans appeared.

eye

ear opening

sharp, serrated teeth

large tongue

huge jaws

clawed fingers

large body

knee

clawed feet

Ancient sea creatures

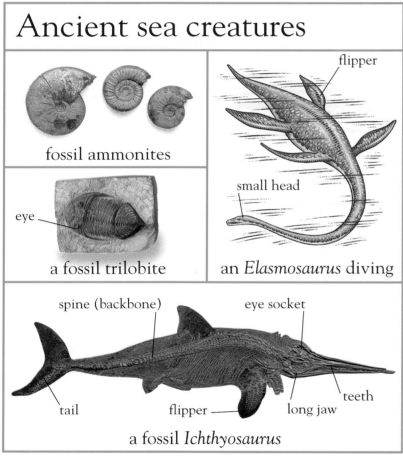

fossil ammonites

eye

a fossil trilobite

flipper

small head

an *Elasmosaurus* diving

spine (backbone)

eye socket

tail

flipper

long jaw

teeth

a fossil *Ichthyosaurus*

Making a replica dinosaur bone

paleontologist

replica (model) bone

Ancient animals

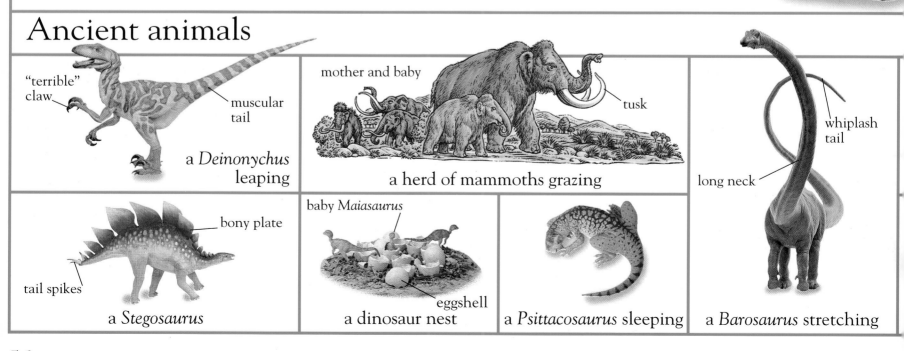

"terrible" claw

muscular tail

a *Deinonychus* leaping

tail spikes

a *Stegosaurus*

mother and baby

tusk

a herd of mammoths grazing

baby *Maiasaurus*

eggshell

a dinosaur nest

a *Psittacosaurus* sleeping

whiplash tail

long neck

a *Barosaurus* stretching

bony plate

A *Tyrannosaurus rex* dinosaur

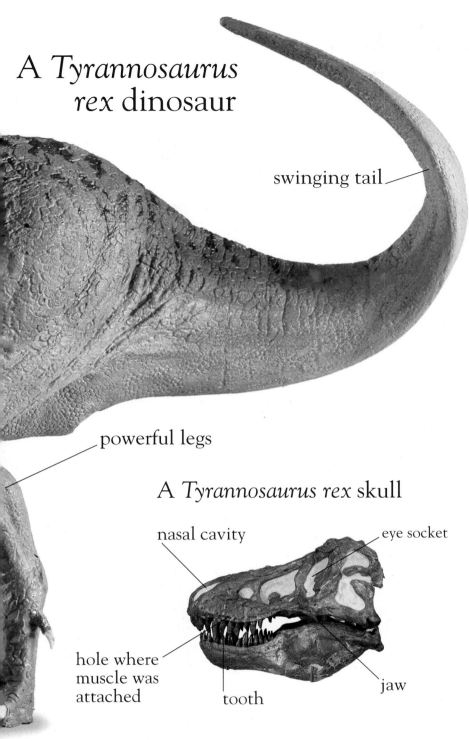

swinging tail

powerful legs

A *Tyrannosaurus rex* skull

nasal cavity

eye socket

hole where muscle was attached

tooth

jaw

Early people

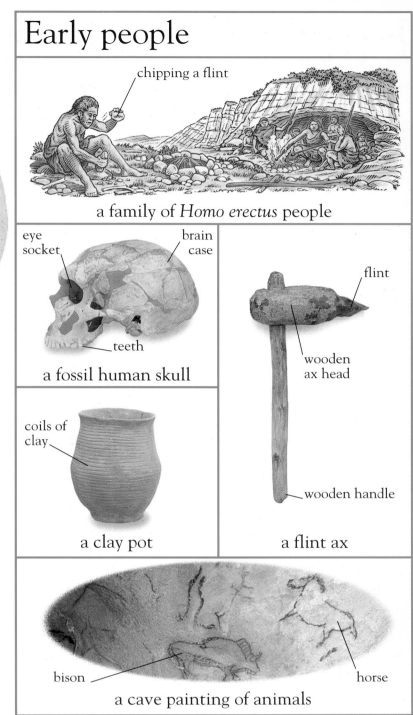

chipping a flint

a family of *Homo erectus* people

eye socket

brain case

teeth

a fossil human skull

flint

wooden ax head

wooden handle

a flint ax

coils of clay

a clay pot

bison

horse

a cave painting of animals

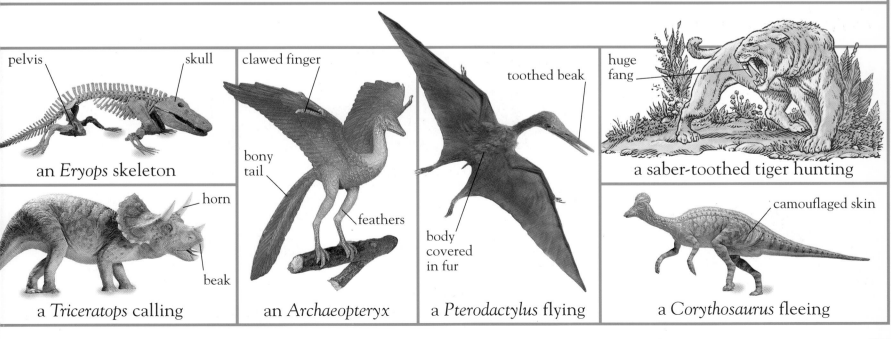

pelvis

skull

an *Eryops* skeleton

horn

beak

a *Triceratops* calling

clawed finger

bony tail

feathers

an *Archaeopteryx*

toothed beak

body covered in fur

a *Pterodactylus* flying

huge fang

a saber-toothed tiger hunting

camouflaged skin

a *Corythosaurus* fleeing

Space

The first artificial satellite was launched into orbit around our planet, Earth, in 1957. Today, different types of spacecraft regularly blast off from Earth. They place satellites into orbit and carry astronauts or equipment such as space probes out into space.

Out in space

a galaxy of stars

an eclipse of the Sun

Sun (behind)

Moon (in front)

a comet

a black hole

a nebula (mist of stars)

a constellation of stars

Planets in our Solar System

Pluto

Neptune

Uranus

Saturn

Jupiter

Mars

Venus

Earth

Mercury

Sun (a star)

An astronaut

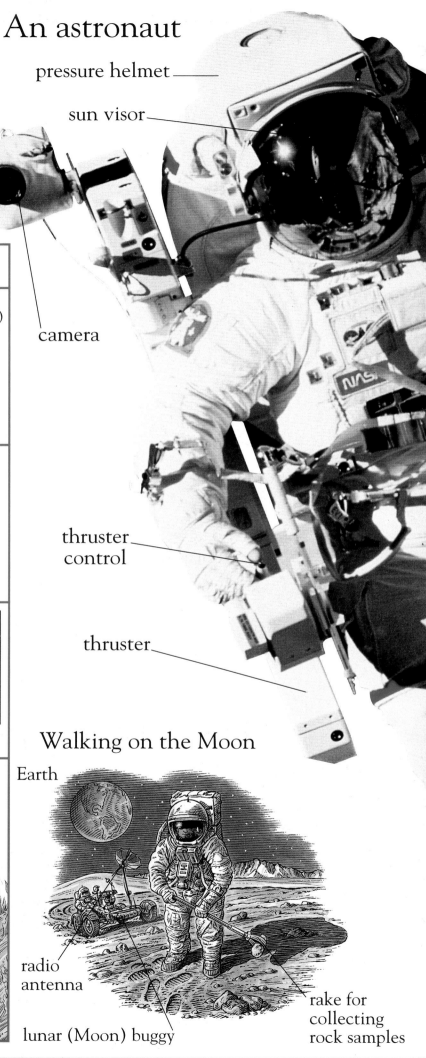

pressure helmet

sun visor

camera

thruster control

thruster

Walking on the Moon

Earth

radio antenna

lunar (Moon) buggy

rake for collecting rock samples

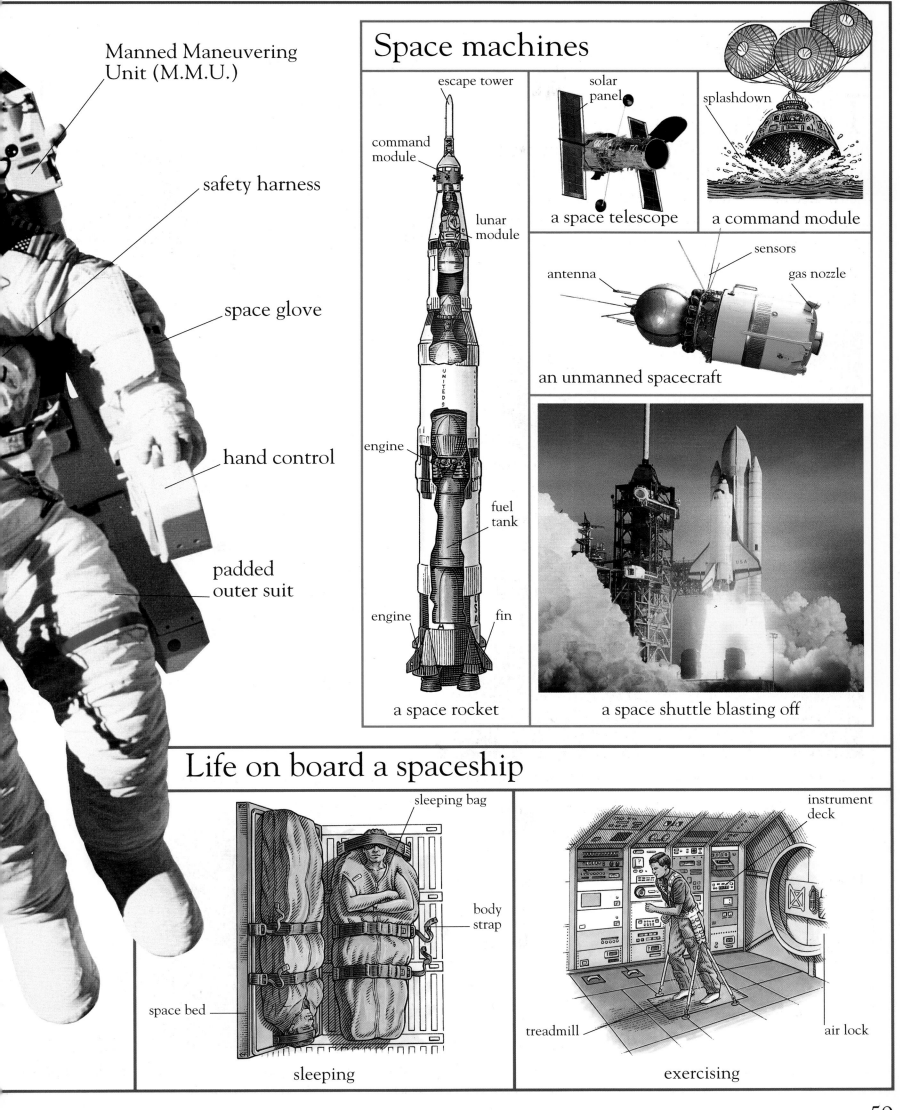

Manned Maneuvering
Unit (M.M.U.)

safety harness

space glove

hand control

padded
outer suit

Space machines

escape tower

command
module

lunar
module

engine

fuel
tank

engine   fin

a space rocket

solar
panel

a space telescope

splashdown

a command module

antenna   sensors

gas nozzle

an unmanned spacecraft

a space shuttle blasting off

Life on board a spaceship

sleeping bag

body
strap

space bed

sleeping

instrument
deck

treadmill   air lock

exercising

Index

T his index shows on which page you can find each word and its picture in this dictionary. You can also use the index to find words and to check spellings when you are writing.

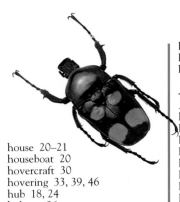

ACKNOWLEDGMENTS

Dorling Kindersley would like to thank the following for their help:

Picture credits
Air 2 Air front cover tr, spine, 33tl; J.Allan Cash 10bl, br, 11bl, 20cl, cb, 21tl, crb, 22br, bl, 23ca, br, bl, 58cbl; Bruce Coleman Ltd/Gerald Cubitt 50tr; Robert Harding Picture Library 11br, 21tr, cl, br, 22–23c, 22bc, 29cla, 52bl, 53bra, 54c, 55tl; Holt Studios/Nigel Catlin 24cla, 25tr, /Mary Cherry 24c; The Hutchison Library 21c, /Bernard Regent 23cra, /M.Von Puttkamer 53tr, 54cl, bl; The Image Bank/Jurgen Vogt 8bl, 10–11c, /Paul J. Sutton 19bc, 21cb, 33trb, bra, /Trevor Wood 51tl, Frank Whitney 54cb, Cliff Feulner 55bcl, /Ira Block 55bcr; London Underground Ltd 29tl; NASA 58–59c, 58bl, 59cr; NHPA 47cr; PGL Adventures 19br; Science Photo Library/NASA 58tl, cl, cla; Tony Stone Images 6bl, br, 22cb, clb, 50bl, 50–51c, 51cra, crb, 51bc, 52tl, cl, br, 53cl, 54tl, bcl, 54–55c, 55cl, tc, tr, ca; Jean Vertut 57cr; World Pictures 51br, 52/53c, 53cl, cr, bc; ZEFA 19bl, 20–21c, 21cr, 23c, 25tl, 29br, 51tr, 55br.

Additional photography
Peter Anderson, Geoff Brightling, Jane Burton, Peter Chadwick, Simon Clay, Andy Crawford, Philip Dowell, John Downes, Mike Dunning, Andreas Von Einsiedel, Neil Fletcher, Lynton Gardiner, Philip Gatward, Frank Greenaway, Finbar Hawkins, John Heseltine, John Holmes, Colin Keates, Dave King, Bob Langrish, Cyril Laubscher, Richard Leeney, John Lepine, Mike Linley, Andrew McRobb, Ray Moller, David Murray, National Maritime Museum, Ian O'Leary, Stephen Oliver, Oxford Scientific Films, Daniel Pangbourne, Roger Phillips, Susanna Price, Barlow Reid, Tim Ridley, David Rudkin, Science Museum, Jules Selmes, Karl Shone, Steve Shott, James Stephenson, Clive Streeter, Kim Taylor, Matthew Ward, Paul Williams, Alex Wilson, Jerry Young.

Models
Sarah Ashun, Jodie Attreed, Jade Bailey, Monica Byles, Hannah Capelton, Jayda Ceylan, Reshmee Doolub, Steve Gorton, Gemmel Haines, James Henderson, Oliver Jenkins, Christina and Luke Kyprianou, Jasmine McAtee, Kim Ng, Peter Radcliffe, Maxwell Ralph, Tebedge Ricketts, John Walden, Martin Wilson.

Additional acknowledgments
Valya Alexander; BBC TV Film Services, Wood Lane, London; Dixon's electrical store; Graphical Innovations for typesetting; Hamleys toystore, 188–196 Regent Street, London, England; picnic hamper on page 13 from John Lewis, Oxford Street, London, England; Lunn Poly Travel Agency; National Meteorological Library, Bracknell, Berkshire, England; Mark Richards; Chris Scollen; Lee Simmons; Martin Wilson.